TABLE OF CO[NTENTS]

DISCLAIMER

INTRODUCTION

Welcome to Liguria
Why Liguria?

CHAPTER ONE

PLANNING YOUR LIGURIA ADVENTURE
1.1 Setting Your Travel Goals
1.2 Choosing the Best Time to Visit
1.3 Visa and Entry Requirements
1.4 Budgeting and Money Matters
1.5 Essential Packing Tips
1.5.1 Travel-friendly luggage options

CHAPTER TWO

GETTING ACQUAINTED LIGURIA
2.1 Historical and Cultural Background
2.2 Languages and Communication
2.3 Currency exchange tips

CHAPTER THREE

CINQUE TERRE - THE JEWEL OF LIGURIA
3.1 Overview of Cinque Terre
3.2 Monterosso al Mare

3.3 Vernazza
3.4 Corniglia
3.5 Manarola
3.6 Riomaggiore
3.7 Hiking Trails and Scenic Routes
3.8 Recommended Restaurants With Their Locations
3.9 Nightclubs and Lounges with their locations

CHAPTER FOUR

GENOA - MARITIME MAJESTY
4.1 Introducing Genoa
4.2 Historical Landmarks and Museums
4.3 Exploring Genoa's Old Town
4.4 The Port of Genoa and Aquarium
4.5 Recommended Restaurants With Their Locations

CHAPTER FIVE

PORTOFINO AND SANTA MARGHERITA LIGURE
5.1 Portofino: A Glamorous Retreat
5.2 Santa Margherita Ligure: Beauty on the Bay
5.3 Outdoor Activities and Waterfront Views
5.4 Elegant Dining and Shopping
5.5 Recommended Restaurant With Their Locations

CHAPTER SIX

THE RIVIERA DI LEVANTE
6.1 Sestri Levante: Bay of Silence and Bay of Fables
6.2 Levanto: Gateway to the Cinque Terre

LIGURIA TRAVEL GUIDE

2024 Edition

Exploring Liguria: Immerse Yourself in Culture, Cuisine, and Natural Beauty along the Italian Riviera

By

Roy McKean

Copyright©2023 Roy McKean

All Right Reserved

6.3 BONASSOLA AND FRAMURA: TRANQUIL RETREATS
6.4 LA SPEZIA: GATEWAY TO THE GULF OF POETS

CHAPTER SEVEN

THE RIVIERA DI PONENTE
7.1 VARIGOTTI AND NOLI: CHARMING COASTAL VILLAGES
7.2 ALBENGA: ANCIENT WONDERS AND CULINARY DELIGHTS
7.3 IMPERIA: OLIVE OIL CAPITAL OF ITALY

CHAPTER EIGHT

THE HINTERLAND - MOUNTAINS AND OLIVE GROVES
8.1 THE LIGURIAN ALPS: NATURE'S PLAYGROUND
8.2 DOLCEACQUA AND APRICALE: MEDIEVAL MAGIC
8.3 TRADITIONAL FESTIVALS AND EVENTS

CHAPTER NINE

NAVIGATING LIGURIA
9.1 TRANSPORTATION OPTIONS
9.1.1 Train Networks: Navigating the Scenic Routes
9.1.2 Local Buses and Taxis: Navigating Urban Centers
9.1.3 Ferry Services: Embracing Coastal Splendor
9.1.4 Car Rentals: Crafting Personal Journeys
9.2 TRAVEL SAFETY TIPS
9.3 TIPS FOR NAVIGATING PUBLIC TRANSPORTATION
9.4 TRAVEL INSURANCE AND ITS IMPORTANCE

CHAPTER TEN

ACCOMMODATION
10.1 HOTELS AND RESORTS
10.2 BOUTIQUE STAYS
10.3 BUDGET-FRIENDLY OPTIONS
10.4 UNIQUE ACCOMMODATION EXPERIENCES
10.5 TIPS FOR FINDING THE RIGHT LODGING FOR YOUR NEEDS

CHAPTER ELEVEN

LIGURIA TRAVEL ITINERARIES
11.1 ONE-WEEK HIGHLIGHTS TOUR
11.2 FAMILY-FRIENDLY ADVENTURE
11.3 SOLO TRAVELER'S JOURNEY
11.4 ROMANTIC GETAWAYS

CHAPTER TWELVE

PRACTICAL TIPS AND RESOURCES
12.1 LOCAL PHRASES AND VOCABULARY
12.2 EMERGENCY CONTACTS
12.3 SUSTAINABLE TRAVEL PRACTICES
12.4 HEALTH PRECAUTIONS

CONCLUSION

REFLECTING ON YOUR LIGURIAN JOURNEY

DISCLAIMER

Welcome to our immersive travel guide! As you embark on this journey through the pages of Liguria travel guide, we want to set clear expectations. While we aim to transport you to captivating destinations and provide valuable insights, we do so without the aid of maps and images.

Why, you ask?

Our intention is simple: to stimulate your imagination and curiosity. By omitting maps, we encourage you to rely on your instincts, engage with locals, and discover hidden gems beyond the well-trodden paths. Instead of images, we invite you to paint vivid mental pictures through words and descriptions, allowing your mind to craft its unique interpretation of the places we explore.

In this text-centric guide, we prioritize storytelling, history, culture, and practical advice. We believe that your own perceptions and interpretations will make your travels more personal and memorable. It's an invitation to be present in the moment, to interact with your surroundings, and to embrace the serendipitous adventures that come your way.

So, as you delve into these pages, let your imagination soar, and let the words be your compass in this world of exploration and discovery.

INTRODUCTION

Welcome to Liguria

Welcome to Liguria, Italy's hidden coastal gem. Nestled in the northwest corner of the country, Liguria is a region of breathtaking natural beauty, rich cultural heritage, and culinary delights. With its picturesque coastline, charming villages, and lush hinterland, Liguria offers a diverse and unforgettable travel experience.

This guide is your passport to discovering the wonders of Liguria. Whether you're drawn to the colorful cliffside villages of Cinque Terre, the maritime majesty of Genoa, or the serene beaches of Santa Margherita Ligure, Liguria has something to captivate every traveler.

As you embark on this journey through Liguria, you'll unravel the layers of history that have shaped this region, from ancient Roman settlements to medieval hilltop towns. You'll savor the flavors of Ligurian cuisine, renowned for its fresh seafood, aromatic herbs, and world-famous pesto.

So, fasten your seatbelt and get ready to explore the coastal paradise that is Liguria. Let the adventure begin!

Why Liguria?

Natural Splendor

Liguria's coastline is nothing short of a masterpiece painted by nature herself. The rugged cliffs of Cinque Terre, the glamorous allure of Portofino, and the pristine beaches along the Riviera di Ponente and Riviera di Levante offer an unparalleled experience for beachgoers, hikers, and nature enthusiasts alike.

Rich Cultural Heritage

Steeped in history, Liguria boasts a tapestry of architectural wonders, ancient ruins, and well-preserved medieval towns. The influence of the maritime republics and the legacy of great explorers are etched into the region's DNA, inviting history buffs to delve into a world of tales from days gone by.

Culinary Delights

Ligurian cuisine is a feast for the senses. From the world-famous pesto sauce to succulent seafood dishes, the region's gastronomy is a celebration of fresh, locally-sourced ingredients. Imagine savoring a plate of trofie pasta drizzled with fragrant basil pesto, accompanied by a glass of crisp local white wine.

Authentic Village Life

Beyond the bustling cities, Liguria's charm lies in its small, authentic villages. Cobblestone streets, pastel-hued houses, and friendly locals create an atmosphere of warmth and hospitality. Whether you're strolling through the narrow alleys of Vernazza or enjoying a gelato in Varigotti, these villages are the heart and soul of Liguria.

Accessibility and Convenience

With well-connected transportation networks, getting around Liguria is a breeze. Trains, buses, and boats link the major towns, making it easy to explore the entire region. Whether you're on a leisurely coastal tour or an adventurous hike, accessibility is never a concern in Liguria.

CHAPTER ONE
PLANNING YOUR LIGURIA ADVENTURE

1.1 Setting Your Travel Goals

Before embarking on your Ligurian adventure, it's essential to invest a little time in setting your travel goals. What is it that you truly wish to experience in this captivating region? Are you envisioning days of blissful relaxation on sun-kissed beaches, where the gentle lull of the waves forms the backdrop to your holiday? Or perhaps you're drawn to the rich tapestry of Liguria's history, eager to wander through ancient streets, absorbing the stories etched into the timeworn facades of its towns and cities. Maybe it's the promise of culinary delight that beckons you, with visions of savoring freshly caught seafood, drizzled in Ligurian olive oil and paired with regional wines.

Defining these aspirations will serve as the compass for your journey, ensuring that every moment in Liguria aligns with your desires. If you seek tranquility, you'll find secluded coves and serene coastal hideaways. If history fascinates you, the region's historical sites and museums will unfold a narrative that spans centuries. And for the gastronomically inclined, Liguria's markets, trattorias, and vineyards stand ready to delight your taste buds.

Moreover, clarifying your objectives empowers you to craft a personalized itinerary, optimizing every day of your Ligurian sojourn. With a clear vision in mind, you can seamlessly blend the leisurely pace of coastal life with explorations of ancient castles and churches. You can schedule moments of culinary revelation, from seaside feasts to intimate, family-run eateries tucked away in narrow alleyways.

In essence, your travel goals are the foundation upon which you'll build cherished memories. They infuse purpose into each step, each choice, and each experience. They're the secret to transforming a vacation into an adventure, and a journey into a soul-enriching odyssey.

So, before you pack your bags and set foot in this coastal paradise, take a moment to reflect on what you seek. Write it down, let it guide you, and watch as Liguria unfolds its treasures in perfect harmony with your aspirations. Your adventure awaits, tailored precisely to your dreams.

1.2 Choosing the Best Time to Visit

Liguria, Italy's coastal gem, is a destination that offers a unique and ever-changing charm with the shifting seasons. The region's allure is multifaceted, and understanding how its character evolves throughout the year can greatly enhance your travel experience.

Summer: Sun-Soaked Beaches and Vibrant Festivals

Liguria in the summer is a vibrant tapestry of colors and experiences. The sun-drenched beaches along the Italian Riviera come alive with sunbathers, water sports enthusiasts, and beachside cafes. It's a season when the coastline truly sparkles, and the crystal-clear waters of the Ligurian Sea beckon for refreshing swims and lazy afternoons.

The summer months, particularly June to August, are also the prime time for numerous festivals and events. Liguria hosts a plethora of traditional celebrations, such as the Palio del Golfo in La Spezia and the Sagra del Pesce (Fish Festival) in Camogli. These events are not only cultural showcases but also vibrant, community-driven gatherings, where you can immerse yourself in the local way of life and savor delicious regional cuisine.

Spring and Autumn: Milder Weather and Fewer Crowds

As spring unfolds, Liguria undergoes a beautiful transformation. The region's landscapes burst into bloom with colorful wildflowers, and the pleasant, mild weather is ideal for outdoor activities. Hiking in the Cinque Terre or exploring the lush hinterland is a delight during this time. With fewer tourists around, you can enjoy the serene beauty of Liguria's natural wonders at your own pace.

Autumn in Liguria is equally enchanting. The weather remains temperate, making it a perfect time for sightseeing and coastal walks. The crowds thin out even further, giving you a more intimate experience of the region's treasures. The changing foliage, particularly in the inland areas, adds another layer of natural beauty to your explorations.

These shoulder seasons—spring (April to June) and autumn (September to October)—are particularly well-suited for those who relish a more tranquil and authentic experience. You'll have the opportunity to interact with locals and savor Liguria's delights without the hustle and bustle of the peak tourist months.

Winter: A Different Kind of Beauty

While Liguria is often associated with summer and the beach, the winter season reveals an entirely different facet of its charm. The coastline may be quieter, but Liguria's appeal remains, with mild winter temperatures and a sense of tranquility that is truly special.

In the winter months, you can explore the historic cities, such as Genoa and La Spezia, without the crowds. The cultural sites, including museums, churches, and historic districts, take on a serene ambiance, allowing for a more intimate connection with the art and history of the region.

Winter is also the ideal time for culinary exploration. Liguria's cuisine is renowned for its comforting, hearty dishes like pesto, farinata, and fresh seafood. The cozy, family-run trattorias and restaurants are perfect for savoring these dishes without the need for reservations.

Moreover, Liguria's scenic landscapes and coastal towns offer their own unique allure in the winter. The dramatic cliffs, picturesque villages, and quiet walks along the promenades take on a peaceful, romantic quality during this time of year. It's an excellent period for those who enjoy a quieter, more reflective travel experience.

Consider Your Preferences and Plan Your Visit Accordingly

When planning your visit to Liguria, it's essential to consider your personal preferences. What kind of experience are you seeking? Do you thrive in the energy of bustling summer beach towns, or do you prefer the tranquility of a less crowded, more authentic experience in spring or autumn? Are you drawn to the charm of Liguria's winter ambiance?

By aligning your travel dates with your desires, you can maximize your enjoyment of this captivating coastal paradise. Each season in Liguria offers its own unique blend of natural beauty, cultural richness, and regional flavors. With careful consideration of your preferences, you can embark on a journey perfectly tailored to your ideal Ligurian adventure.

1.3 Visa and Entry Requirements

If you're planning a visit to this enchanting destination, it's crucial to be well-informed about the visa and entry requirements. This comprehensive guide will walk you through the essential information you need to ensure a smooth and hassle-free entry into Liguria.

Understanding Schengen Visa Regulations

Liguria is part of the Schengen Area, an agreement among 26 European countries that allows for passport-free travel across their shared borders. If you're a citizen of a country outside the Schengen Area, you may need to obtain a Schengen visa to enter Liguria.

Who Needs a Schengen Visa?

Citizens of certain countries are required to obtain a Schengen visa before entering the Schengen Area, including Liguria. The list of visa-required countries may change, so it's crucial to check with the official consulate or embassy for the most up-to-date information.

Visa Types and Duration

Schengen visas come in various types, including tourist visas, business visas, and transit visas. For tourists, a short-stay visa (Type C) is typically applicable. This allows you to stay in the Schengen Area for up to 90 days within a 180-day period.

Application Process and Documentation

Obtaining a Schengen visa involves a structured application process and requires specific documentation. Here's what you'll need:

1. Visa Application Form:

You must complete a Schengen visa application form. This form can usually be downloaded from the official website of the consulate or embassy handling visa applications.

2. Passport:

Your passport must be valid for at least three months beyond your planned departure from the Schengen Area. It should also have at least two blank pages for visa stamps.

3. Passport-sized Photos:

You'll need recent passport-sized photos that meet Schengen visa photo requirements. These are usually 35mm x 45mm with a white background.

4. Travel Itinerary:

Provide a detailed itinerary of your trip, including flight reservations, accommodation bookings, and planned activities in Liguria.

5. Proof of Accommodation:

Include confirmation of your hotel reservations or any other type of lodging you've arranged for your stay in Liguria.

6. Travel Insurance:

You must have travel insurance that covers at least €30,000 in medical expenses and repatriation for the entire duration of your stay in the Schengen Area.

7. Financial Means:

You should provide proof of sufficient financial means to cover your stay, including bank statements, pay stubs, or any other relevant financial documentation.

8. Visa Fee:

A non-refundable visa fee is required upon application. The fee amount may vary depending on your nationality and the type of visa you're applying for.

9. Additional Documents:

Depending on your specific circumstances (such as employment status, purpose of visit, etc.), you may be required to submit additional documents. These could include an employment letter, invitation letter, proof of enrollment (for students), or other relevant documents.

Visa Processing Time

The processing time for a Schengen visa application can vary depending on your nationality, the consulate's workload, and the time of year. It's advisable to apply for your visa well in advance of your planned travel dates, preferably at least 3 to 4 weeks prior.

Visa Interview

In some cases, you may be required to attend a visa interview at the consulate or embassy. This interview is an opportunity for the visa officer to assess the authenticity of your application and to ask any additional questions they may have.

Entry Requirements for Non-Visa Nationals

Some countries have agreements with the Schengen Area that exempt their citizens from requiring a Schengen visa for short stays. However, even if you're from a visa-exempt country, you'll still need to meet certain entry requirements, including:

Valid Passport: Ensure your passport is valid for at least three months beyond your planned departure from the Schengen Area.

Purpose of Visit: Clearly state the purpose of your visit, whether it's tourism, business, or other acceptable reasons.

Sufficient Funds: Be able to demonstrate that you have enough money to cover your expenses during your stay.

Return Ticket: Have a confirmed return ticket or proof of onward travel.

Proof of Accommodation: Provide confirmation of your accommodation arrangements.

Travel Insurance: It's advisable to have travel insurance, even if not mandatory.

Final Considerations

While this guide provides a comprehensive overview of visa and entry requirements for tourists visiting Liguria, it's important to remember that regulations may change, and individual circumstances can vary. Therefore, it's highly recommended to check with the official consulate or embassy well in advance of your travel dates to ensure you have the most up-to-date and accurate information.

By being well-prepared and organized in your visa application process, you can embark on your Ligurian adventure with confidence, knowing that you have met all the necessary requirements for a memorable and enjoyable stay in this breathtaking region of Italy.

1.4 Budgeting and Money Matters

Touring the picturesque region of Liguria can be an unforgettable experience, but wise budgeting and financial planning are crucial for a successful and stress-free journey. Whether you're a backpacker on a tight budget or a luxury traveler seeking the finer things in life, here's a comprehensive guide to help you manage your finances while exploring Liguria.

1. Calculate Your Trip Costs

Before you set foot in Liguria, it's essential to have a clear understanding of the costs involved in your journey. This includes your accommodation, transportation, meals, activities, and any extras such as shopping or souvenirs. Doing your research and estimating these expenses will give you a baseline for your budget.

2. Accommodation Options

Liguria offers a wide range of accommodation options to suit various budgets. From luxury hotels to boutique guesthouses and budget-friendly hostels, you'll find choices that fit your financial comfort zone. Booking in advance, especially during peak tourist seasons, can often secure better rates.

3. Dining and Cuisine Highlights

Ligurian cuisine is a delight for the senses, and it's essential to allocate a portion of your budget for food. While there are high-end restaurants with Michelin stars, you can also savor authentic Ligurian dishes in local trattorias and osterias that are budget-friendly. Be sure to try the regional specialty, pesto, and fresh seafood dishes. For cost-conscious travelers, markets offer fresh produce and snacks for picnics.

4. Transportation Costs

Liguria is well-connected by trains, buses, and boats, making it easy to explore the region. Plan your journeys wisely and consider purchasing rail passes or regional transportation cards for potential savings. Additionally, walking and hiking are popular activities in Liguria and can be both budget-friendly and rewarding.

5. Tips for Budget-Conscious Travelers

- Opt for Local Eateries: Dining in local restaurants and cafes is often more affordable than tourist-centric venues. Try the daily specials for a taste of local flavors.
- Use Public Transportation: Trains and buses are not only convenient but also economical ways to travel between towns and cities. Consider multi-journey passes for additional savings.
- Enjoy Free Activities: Liguria's natural beauty is a gift that keeps on giving. Spend your days on the beach, explore charming streets, and take advantage of free or low-cost activities, such as hiking or visiting public gardens and parks.

6. Currency Exchange and Payment Methods

The official currency in Italy is the Euro (EUR). It's advisable to exchange currency at banks or exchange offices for better rates compared to airport currency exchange counters. Additionally, notify your bank about your travel plans to avoid any issues with using your credit or debit cards abroad.

7. Emergency Fund

It's always a good practice to have an emergency fund set aside for unexpected expenses. This can include medical costs, lost or stolen items, or any unforeseen travel disruptions. Having peace of mind with a financial safety net ensures a stress-free experience.

Budgeting and money management play a pivotal role in ensuring a smooth and enjoyable trip to Liguria. By calculating your expenses, choosing the right accommodation and dining options, and being mindful of transportation costs, you can make the most of your Ligurian adventure without breaking the bank. Remember, with proper financial planning, you can relish the stunning beauty, rich culture, and delectable cuisine Liguria has to offer, making your journey a memorable one.

1.5 Essential Packing Tips

Packing for your Ligurian escapade requires a blend of practicality and preparedness to ensure you make the most of this coastal paradise. Here are some crucial tips to help you pack smart and enjoy every moment of your journey:

1. Weather-Appropriate Attire:

Liguria experiences varying climates. If you're visiting in the warmer months, pack lightweight, breathable fabrics like cotton and linen. For spring or autumn, layers are key to adapt to changing temperatures. Don't forget a light jacket or sweater for cooler evenings.

2. Comfortable Footwear:

Whether you're strolling through historic towns, hiking the Cinque Terre trails, or simply exploring the coastline, comfortable walking shoes are a must. Consider packing a pair of sturdy sneakers or lightweight hiking shoes.

3. Swimwear and Beach Essentials:

If you plan to soak up the sun on Liguria's stunning beaches, pack your favorite swimwear, a beach towel, sunscreen, and a wide-brimmed hat for added sun protection.

4. Sun Protection and Hydration:

Liguria's sunny climate calls for ample sun protection. Pack a high SPF sunscreen, sunglasses, and a reusable water bottle to stay hydrated, especially during outdoor activities.

5. Modest Attire for Visiting Churches and Historical Sites:

If you plan on visiting churches or historical sites, it's respectful to have attire that covers your shoulders and knees. A light shawl or scarf can be a handy addition to your daypack.

6. Daypack or Small Backpack:

A small backpack or daypack is invaluable for carrying essentials like water, snacks, a camera, a light jacket, and any items you pick up along the way.

7. Power Adapters and Electronics:

Liguria uses the European standard plug (Type C and F). Don't forget to bring a power adapter if your devices have a different plug type. Remember to pack chargers, a power bank, and any necessary electronics for capturing memories.

8. Toiletries and Personal Care Items:

While you can find most toiletries in Liguria, it's advisable to bring your preferred brands. Include items like shampoo, conditioner, toothbrush, toothpaste, and any special skincare products you may need.

9. Travel Documents and Copies:

Ensure you have all necessary travel documents, including your passport, visa (if required), travel insurance, and any printed reservations. Keep digital copies stored securely in case of emergencies.

10. Language and Guide Books:

While many in Liguria speak English, having a basic Italian phrasebook or a translation app can be incredibly helpful and appreciated by locals.

11. Medications and First Aid Kit:

If you have specific medications or medical requirements, ensure you have an ample supply for the duration of your trip. It's also wise to carry a basic first aid kit for minor emergencies.

12. Adaptable Clothing for Different Activities:

Plan outfits that can transition from daytime exploration to evening dining. Consider items like versatile dresses or shirts that can be dressed up or down.

1.5.1 Travel-friendly luggage options

Selecting the right luggage is a crucial aspect of ensuring a smooth and enjoyable trip to Liguria. Your choice of luggage can significantly impact your mobility and comfort during your travels. Here are some travel-friendly luggage options to consider:

1. Wheeled Suitcases:

Advantages: Wheeled suitcases are a popular choice for travelers due to their ease of maneuverability. They come in various sizes, from compact carry-ons to larger checked bags, allowing you to tailor your luggage to the length of your stay.

Considerations: Opt for suitcases with sturdy, multidirectional wheels for easy navigation through airports, train stations, and city streets. Additionally, choose a suitcase with a durable shell to protect your belongings.

2. Travel Backpacks:

Advantages: Travel backpacks offer versatility and are well-suited for those planning to explore on foot or use public transportation. They typically have multiple compartments for organized packing.

Considerations: Look for backpacks with padded shoulder straps and a comfortable hip belt to distribute the weight evenly. Consider models with a detachable daypack for added convenience during day trips.

3. Duffel Bags with Wheels:

Advantages: Wheeled duffel bags combine the flexibility of a duffel with the convenience of wheels. They are excellent for travelers who want the option to carry their luggage or roll it.

Considerations: Opt for a duffel bag with durable wheels and reinforced handles for easy lifting. Look for a water-resistant material to protect your belongings in case of rain.

4. Carry-On Luggage:

Advantages: Carry-ons are compact, making them an excellent choice for short trips or for those who prefer to travel light. They can be easily stowed in overhead compartments on planes and trains.

Considerations: Ensure your carry-on meets the size requirements of your chosen airline or transportation method. Look for features like built-in USB ports for charging devices on the go.

5. Hybrid Backpack-Rolling Bags:

Advantages: These innovative designs combine the benefits of a backpack and a rolling suitcase. They are versatile, allowing you to switch between carrying and rolling as needed.

Considerations: Look for models with comfortable backpack straps that can be easily stowed when not in use. Ensure the wheels and handles are durable and suitable for various terrains.

6. Packing Cubes and Organizers:

Advantages: While not luggage per se, packing cubes and organizers help keep your belongings neat and organized within your chosen luggage. They're especially useful for separating clean clothes from dirty laundry and for easy access to specific items.

Considerations: Choose lightweight yet durable packing cubes that fit well within your luggage. Opt for mesh or breathable fabric to allow for ventilation.

When selecting your luggage, consider the nature of your trip, the activities you plan to engage in, and your personal preferences for carrying or rolling your belongings. Additionally, prioritize durability and functionality to ensure your luggage serves you well throughout your Ligurian adventure.

CHAPTER TWO
GETTING ACQUAINTED LIGURIA

2.1 Historical and Cultural Background

Liguria, cradled along the northwest coast of Italy, is a region steeped in a rich tapestry of history and culture. Its origins trace back to ancient times when it was inhabited by the Ligures, a Celtic tribe known for their resilience and distinct way of life. Over the centuries, Liguria evolved, and with its strategic coastal location, it became a sought-after territory for various empires.

As the Ligures navigated their way through history, Liguria eventually transformed into a Roman province, leaving behind enduring traces of Roman influence in its architecture and traditions. The remnants of ancient Roman settlements still dot the landscape, reminding visitors of this region's deep historical roots.

The maritime heritage of Liguria stands as a testament to its importance in Italy's nautical history. Coastal towns such as Genoa, La Spezia, and Savona flourished as vital trading ports during the Middle Ages and the Renaissance. Among these, Genoa emerged as a dominant maritime republic, rivalling the likes of Venice and Pisa. Its powerful fleet and strategic alliances allowed it to control vast stretches of the Mediterranean, leaving a lasting mark on Liguria's identity.

Wandering through Liguria's coastal towns, one can't help but be enraptured by the grandeur of the past. Magnificent palaces and fortifications, once the epicenters of maritime trade and diplomacy, now stand as silent witnesses to Liguria's storied past. The imposing stone walls and elegant facades whisper tales of bygone eras, evoking a sense of awe and wonder.

In modern times, Liguria continues to hold its cultural traditions close to heart. The people of Liguria embrace their heritage with fervor, infusing every corner of the region with a palpable sense of pride. Vibrant festivals, a blend of ancient rites and modern revelry, fill the calendar, celebrating saints, maritime achievements, and the enduring spirit of the Ligurian people.

Music and dance play an integral role in Ligurian culture, reflecting the rhythm of life along the coast. Traditional tunes resonate through cobbled streets, their melodies weaving stories of love, labor, and seafaring adventures. Folk dances, with their spirited steps and lively rhythms, animate town squares, inviting both locals and visitors to partake in the joyous celebration of Liguria's living heritage.

Liguria's cultural vibrancy is not confined to grand spectacles alone. It permeates daily life, from the rustic trattorias serving time-honored recipes passed down through generations, to the bustling markets where vendors proudly offer their wares, each telling a story of the land and sea. Even a casual stroll through a Ligurian village reveals intricately carved doorways, colorful facades, and charming courtyards—a living canvas that pays homage to a time when craftsmanship was a cherished art.

2.2 Languages and Communication

Italian serves as the official language of Liguria, threading through the conversations and interactions of its inhabitants. Yet, due to Liguria's geographical proximity to France and its historical interactions with neighboring regions, the lilting cadence of French can also be heard, particularly in the border areas. This linguistic blend adds a unique dimension to Liguria's cultural mosaic, illustrating the interconnectedness of this coastal haven with its European counterparts.

In the bustling hubs frequented by tourists, English emerges as a widely spoken lingua franca. The cosmopolitan atmosphere of these areas fosters a multilingual environment, ensuring that travelers from around the world can navigate with relative ease. However, there's an unspoken warmth that emanates when visitors take the extra step to communicate in Italian. It's a gesture that resonates deeply with the Ligurian people, evoking a sense of camaraderie and appreciation for the effort put forth.

To truly unlock the heart of Liguria, consider immersing yourself in a handful of basic Italian phrases. These linguistic keys serve as bridges, not only allowing you to navigate the practicalities of travel but also opening doors to meaningful connections with the locals. A warm "Buongiorno" in the morning, a sincere "Grazie" for a kind gesture, or a heartfelt "Arrivederci" as you bid farewell—these simple expressions carry the spirit of Liguria within them. They forge a link between you and the warm-hearted Ligurian community, leaving an indelible mark on your travel experience. So, embrace the language, and let it become a companion on your journey through this captivating coastal paradise.

2.3 Currency exchange tips

When visiting Liguria, understanding the currency exchange process is essential for a smooth and hassle-free experience. Here are some valuable currency exchange tips for tourists:

1. Know the Official Currency: The official currency of Italy, including Liguria, is the Euro (€). It is widely accepted throughout the region in shops, restaurants, and other establishments.

2. Exchange a Small Amount in Advance: If you're arriving with foreign currency, it's advisable to exchange a small amount at the airport or in major cities to cover initial expenses like transportation and meals. However, keep in mind that exchange rates at airports and high-tourist areas may not be as favorable as in local banks.

3. Use ATMs for Convenience: ATMs are readily available in cities, towns, and even smaller villages in Liguria. They offer the convenience of withdrawing cash in the local currency as needed. Look for ATMs affiliated with major international networks like Visa and Mastercard for the widest acceptance.

4. Check with Your Bank: Before departing for Liguria, inform your bank of your travel plans. This prevents any unexpected issues with your credit or debit cards being blocked due to international transactions. Additionally, inquire about any foreign transaction fees or ATM withdrawal charges that may apply.

5. Monitor Exchange Rates: Keep an eye on currency exchange rates leading up to your trip. This can help you identify favorable times to exchange your money. There are several reliable websites and mobile apps available that provide up-to-date exchange rate information.

6. Consider Using Credit and Debit Cards: Major credit and debit cards are widely accepted in Liguria, especially in hotels, restaurants, and larger stores. They offer a convenient and secure way to make purchases. However, it's always good to have some cash on hand for smaller establishments or places that may not accept cards.

7. Beware of Dynamic Currency Conversion (DCC): When using your credit card for transactions in Liguria, you may be offered the option of paying in your home currency. This is known as Dynamic Currency Conversion (DCC). While it may seem convenient, it often comes with unfavorable exchange rates. It's usually more cost-effective to choose to pay in the local currency.

8. Keep Emergency Cash: While Liguria is generally card-friendly, it's wise to keep a small amount of cash on hand for emergencies or for places that may not accept cards.

By following these currency exchange tips, you'll be well-prepared to navigate the financial aspects of your Ligurian adventure, ensuring a seamless and enjoyable travel experience.

CHAPTER THREE

CINQUE TERRE - THE JEWEL OF LIGURIA

3.1 Overview of Cinque Terre

Nestled along the rugged coastline of Liguria, Cinque Terre emerges as a jewel in Italy's crown of coastal treasures. This extraordinary destination holds the esteemed title of a UNESCO World Heritage Site, a testament to its exceptional natural beauty and cultural significance. Comprising five distinct villages, each with its own beguiling character, Cinque Terre invites travelers to step back in time and experience the unhurried rhythms of a coastal existence.

The villages of Monterosso al Mare, Vernazza, Corniglia, Manarola, and Riomaggiore stand like colorful sentinels against the azure backdrop of the Ligurian Sea. Each settlement tells a unique story, from the lively beaches of Monterosso to the perched tranquility of Corniglia. The sense of community is palpable, with generations of families weaving their lives into the very fabric of these villages, creating a warm and welcoming atmosphere for all who venture here.

Wandering through the cobbled streets of these coastal hamlets, visitors are transported to a time when life unfolded at a more leisurely pace. Weather-worn facades draped in cascades of vibrant bougainvillaea greet explorers at every turn. The scent of salt-laden air mingles with the aroma of local specialties wafting from charming trattorias and family-run eateries. Each narrow alleyway reveals a new vista, whether it be a glimpse of the shimmering sea or a secret garden tucked away behind ancient stone walls.

Cinque Terre embodies a philosophy of sustainable living, where the natural world coexists harmoniously with human habitation. The iconic terraced vineyards, painstakingly carved into the steep hillsides, speak to the ingenuity and tenacity of the local people. These terraces not only produce some of Italy's finest wines but also serve as a living testament to the profound connection between humanity and the land.

For the intrepid explorer, Cinque Terre offers more than just quaint villages and picturesque vistas. The network of well-marked hiking trails crisscrossing the rugged terrain provides an opportunity to immerse oneself in the breathtaking scenery. As you traverse these ancient pathways, you'll encounter panoramic viewpoints that unveil the true majesty of this coastal enclave.

In Cinque Terre, simplicity reigns supreme, and the genuine warmth of the locals embraces every visitor. Whether you're savoring the catch of the day in a seaside trattoria or strolling along the centuries-old quays, you'll find a profound sense of connection to a way of life that is both timeless and eternally captivating. This UNESCO World Heritage Site stands not only as a testament to the past but also as an enduring invitation to all who seek the serenity of a coastal paradise.

3.2 Monterosso al Mare

Nestled along the enchanting coastline of Liguria, Monterosso al Mare emerges as a beacon of coastal charm.

As the largest and oldest of the five villages comprising Cinque Terre, Monterosso offers a unique blend of historical richness and modern amenities, making it an ideal destination for travelers seeking a quintessential Italian coastal experience.

History and Heritage

Monterosso's origins can be traced back to Roman times, and remnants of this ancient past can still be glimpsed in the old town's architecture. The village has weathered the centuries, surviving pirate raids and natural disasters to stand today as a testament to the resilience of its inhabitants.

Points of Interest

1. Monterosso Beaches:

Monterosso is renowned for its picturesque beaches. Divided into two main sections, the Fegina and Old Town beaches, visitors can bask in the Ligurian sun, take a dip in the clear blue waters, or simply relax on the golden sands. Sunbeds and umbrellas are available for rent, ensuring a comfortable day by the sea.

2. Giant Statue and Trails:

The iconic Giant statue, Il Gigante, carved into the cliffs overlooking Monterosso, is a must-see. It stands as both a marvel of engineering and a symbol of Monterosso's enduring spirit. Nearby, hikers can embark on the renowned Sentiero Azzurro trail, part of the extensive network of hiking paths connecting the Cinque Terre villages.

3. San Francesco Church:

This historic church, dating back to the 17th century, is a captivating blend of Gothic and Ligurian styles. Inside, visitors can admire exquisite frescoes and a striking rose window.

4. Convent of the Capuchin Friars:

Nestled high on a hill, this ancient convent offers breathtaking panoramic views of Monterosso and its surroundings. The climb is rewarded with a serene atmosphere and stunning vistas.

5. Lemon Groves:

Liguria is renowned for its lemons, and Monterosso boasts some of the finest lemon groves in the region. Take a leisurely stroll through these fragrant orchards and savor the sights and scents of this quintessential Ligurian landscape.

Activities

1. Water Sports:

For those seeking adventure, Monterosso offers a range of water sports, from kayaking to paddleboarding. Rental shops along the beachfront provide all the necessary equipment.

2. Wine Tasting:

Liguria is celebrated for its wines, and Monterosso is no exception. Visit local wineries to sample the region's distinctive white wines, including the renowned Cinque Terre DOC.

3. Cooking Classes:

Immerse yourself in Ligurian cuisine by participating in a cooking class. Learn to prepare traditional dishes like pesto, trofie pasta, and seafood specialties.

Dining in Monterosso

Monterosso's culinary scene is a delightful reflection of its coastal setting. Seafood takes center stage, with fresh catches of the day gracing the menus of local trattorias. Don't miss the chance to indulge in Liguria's culinary jewel: pesto. Made from fresh basil, pine nuts, garlic, Parmesan, and olive oil, it's a taste of pure Mediterranean delight.

Recommended Restaurants:

- Ristorante Miky: Via Fegina, 104, 19016 Monterosso al Mare SP
- Il Casello: Via IV Novembre, 4, 19016 Monterosso al Mare SP
- Al Pozzo: Via Roma, 24, 19016 Monterosso al Mare SP

3.3 Vernazza

Nestled on the Ligurian coast, Vernazza is a jewel in the crown of Italy's Cinque Terre, a UNESCO World Heritage Site. This enchanting village, with its colorful houses clinging to the cliffs, welcomes visitors with open arms. Vernazza encapsulates the essence of a Mediterranean idyll, boasting a rich tapestry of history, stunning landscapes, and an inviting atmosphere that beckons travelers from around the world.

History and Heritage

Vernazza's history is woven into its very stone, evident in the remnants of medieval fortifications and ancient churches. The imposing Doria Castle, perched dramatically above the village, stands as a testament to Vernazza's strategic significance in centuries past. From this vantage point, visitors are rewarded with sweeping views of the emerald sea and the rugged coastline, reminding us of the village's maritime heritage.

Quaint Charm and Architecture

As you meander through Vernazza's narrow alleyways, you'll be greeted by the sight of charming houses painted in vibrant hues of ochre, peach, and terracotta. Bougainvillaea spill over balconies, infusing the air with a heady fragrance, and cats laze in the sun-dappled squares. The waterfront is lined with small fishing boats bobbing gently on the waves, offering a glimpse into the traditional way of life that still thrives here.

The Harbor and Seaside Promenade

Vernazza's picturesque harbor is the heart of the village, a place where locals and visitors alike converge to soak in the maritime atmosphere. Fishing boats sway gently, their vibrant colors mirroring the buildings along the shore. The small sandy beach, though modest in size, invites sunseekers to relax and take in the serene beauty that surrounds them.

A leisurely stroll along the seaside promenade reveals a tableau of postcard-worthy scenes. Cafés and restaurants spill out onto the waterfront, offering an ideal spot to savor a leisurely meal while the sea breeze carries the scent of salt and fresh catch. Watching the sun dip below the horizon, casting a golden hue over the village, is a moment etched in memory.

The Church of Santa Margherita d'Antiochia

At the heart of Vernazza stands the Church of Santa Margherita d'Antiochia, a testament to the enduring spiritual significance of this coastal haven. This Romanesque-style church, with its distinctive striped facade, dates back to the 14th century. Step inside to find a tranquil space adorned with centuries-old frescoes and a sense of reverence that transcends time.

Culinary Delights

Vernazza's gastronomy is a celebration of the sea's bounty. Local trattorias serve up delectable dishes that showcase the freshest catches of the day. Anchovies, a regional specialty, take center stage in a variety of preparations, from marinated to deep-fried, offering a true taste of the Ligurian coast. Pesto, made from locally grown basil, is another culinary treasure not to be missed.

Hiking Trails and Adventure

For the intrepid traveler, Vernazza is a gateway to the extensive network of hiking trails that crisscross the Cinque Terre National Park. The famous Sentiero Azzurro (Blue Trail) connects all five villages, offering breathtaking views of the coastline. The challenging yet rewarding trek to Monterosso al Mare is a must for avid hikers, while the Via dell'Amore trail to Manarola is a romantic route perfect for couples.

Local Events and Festivals

Throughout the year, Vernazza comes alive with a calendar of lively events and festivals that showcase the vibrant culture of the region. The Feast of Santa Margherita, celebrated in July, pays tribute to the patron saint of the village with processions, music, and traditional food. The annual Wine Festival in September is a joyous occasion to sample the renowned wines of Cinque Terre.

In Vernazza, time seems to slow, allowing visitors to savor every moment of their coastal sojourn. Whether you're exploring ancient fortifications, savoring local delicacies, or simply gazing out at the endless expanse of the Ligurian Sea, Vernazza offers an experience that transcends the ordinary. This village, steeped in history and bathed in natural beauty, invites you to become a part of its enduring story.

3.4 Corniglia

Nestled on the cliffs of the Italian Riviera, Corniglia stands as a hidden gem among the famous Cinque Terre villages. Often overshadowed by its more bustling neighbors, Corniglia's charm lies in its serene beauty, unspoiled authenticity, and panoramic views of the Ligurian Sea. For travelers seeking an authentic Italian coastal experience, Corniglia is a must-visit destination.

Getting to Corniglia

Access to Corniglia is a bit different from other Cinque Terre villages due to its elevated position. To reach Corniglia, you can:

- Train: The most common method is to take a train to Corniglia's railway station. The village is well-connected by train to the other Cinque Terre towns and major cities like La Spezia and Genoa.
- Car: If you're driving, there's a small parking area outside the village. However, parking is limited, and spaces may fill up quickly during peak tourist season.
- Hiking: For the more adventurous traveler, you can hike from neighboring villages. The famous "Lover's Lane" (Via dell'Amore) connects Manarola and Corniglia, providing a scenic walk with stunning views.

Exploring Corniglia

Corniglia is distinct from its sister villages in many ways. It's perched on a promontory, offering commanding vistas of the Mediterranean. As you explore this picturesque town, here are some points of interest you won't want to miss:

1. Chiesa di San Pietro (Church of San Peter)

Corniglia's historic center is dominated by the Chiesa di San Pietro, a charming 14th-century church with a stunning rose window. Climb the steps to the church's terrace for breathtaking views of the village and sea. It's a perfect spot for photos and taking in the serene atmosphere.

2. Terraced Vineyards

The lush vineyards surrounding Corniglia are a sight to behold. These terraced slopes have been cultivated for centuries, producing exquisite white wines, particularly the local specialty, Vernaccia. Take a stroll through the vineyards for a closer look and enjoy the tranquility of the countryside.

3. Town Square (Piazza Largo Taragio)

Corniglia's main square is a delightful place to relax and soak in the local atmosphere. You'll find charming cafés and restaurants here, perfect for enjoying Ligurian cuisine and a glass of the famous Vernaccia wine. It's a great spot to unwind after a day of exploring.

4. Scenic Balconies

One of Corniglia's unique features is its numerous scenic balconies overlooking the sea. As you explore the village, you'll encounter several viewpoints that provide stunning panoramic views of the coastline. These spots are ideal for taking in the natural beauty and capturing the perfect vacation photos.

5. Corniglia's Beach

Although Corniglia isn't directly on the waterfront like some of the other Cinque Terre villages, it does have a hidden gem known as Guvano Beach. Accessible via a challenging path, this secluded beach offers a more private and wild experience for those seeking to relax by the sea.

6. Hiking Trails

Corniglia serves as a central point for hikers, with multiple trails connecting it to other Cinque Terre villages. In addition to the Via dell'Amore, you can explore routes like the Sentiero Azzurro (Blue Trail) and the scenic hike to Vernazza. These trails provide opportunities to experience the breathtaking natural beauty of the region.

7. Vernaccia Tasting

Don't leave Corniglia without trying the local white wine, Vernaccia. Many of the village's wine shops and restaurants offer wine tastings, allowing you to savor the unique flavors of this regional specialty.

Travel Tips for Corniglia

- Local Delicacies: Be sure to try local specialties like anchovies, pesto, and focaccia while dining in Corniglia's charming restaurants.
- Limited Accommodation: Corniglia has fewer accommodations compared to some other Cinque Terre villages, so it's advisable to book your stay in advance, especially during peak tourist seasons.
- Limited Nightlife: Unlike some of the more bustling Cinque Terre villages, Corniglia is quieter in the evenings. While you can enjoy a serene dinner and a relaxing evening, don't expect a vibrant nightlife scene.
- Respect the Environment: As with all Cinque Terre, be mindful of the environment. Stay on marked paths

when hiking, dispose of your waste responsibly, and respect local customs and traditions.

Corniglia may not have the same frenetic energy as its neighbors, but that's precisely its charm. It offers a tranquil, unspoiled slice of Italian coastal life that captivates visitors with its stunning natural beauty and quiet authenticity. Whether you're hiking through vineyards, sipping Vernaccia wine, or simply enjoying the Mediterranean breeze, Corniglia is a destination that embodies the essence of Cinque Terre and Liguria.

3.5 Manarola

Manarola, a captivating village perched on the cliffs of the Ligurian coast, is one of the five charming towns that make up Cinque Terre. Known for its dramatic landscapes, colorful buildings, and rich maritime heritage, Manarola is a must-visit destination for travelers seeking an authentic Italian coastal experience.

Getting to Manarola

Manarola is well-connected to other Cinque Terre towns, making it accessible by train, car, and even on foot for the adventurous hiker.

- By Train: The most convenient way to reach Manarola is by train. The Cinque Terre train line connects all five villages, with regular services running from La Spezia to Levanto. Manarola's train station is right in the heart of the village, allowing for easy access to the town and its attractions.

- By Car: While driving to Manarola is possible, parking can be challenging due to the limited space available in the village. It's recommended to park in La Spezia or Levanto and then take the train to Manarola.
- Hiking: Manarola is part of the scenic Blue Trail that connects all five Cinque Terre villages. Hikers can enjoy breathtaking views while trekking from one town to another. The Manarola to Riomaggiore section of the trail, known as the Via dell'Amore, is a popular and relatively easy hike.

The Charm of Manarola

Manarola exudes an old-world charm that immediately captures the hearts of visitors. The village's unique character is a blend of natural beauty, rich history, and the warmth of its residents.

Colorful Buildings:

One of the most iconic features of Manarola is its colorful buildings that cling to the cliffs overlooking the Mediterranean Sea. The vibrant hues of orange, yellow, and pink create a stunning contrast against the azure waters. These colorful facades are not just for aesthetics; they help fishermen identify their homes from the sea.

Historical Sites:

Manarola boasts several historical sites that provide a glimpse into its past. The Church of San Lorenzo, a 14th-century Gothic church, stands proudly in the town square. Its black and white striped facade and ornate rose window are architectural marvels. Nearby, the Oratorio dei

Disciplinati, a small chapel, showcases exquisite artwork and hosts local religious events.

Scenic Beauty:

Manarola's natural beauty is awe-inspiring. The rugged coastline and terraced vineyards, called "cian," have been meticulously crafted over centuries. These terraces not only produce the famous Manarola wine but also serve as a reminder of the ingenuity and determination of the local people.

The Marina:

Manarola features a picturesque marina with colorful boats bobbing in the crystal-clear waters. It's a great place to watch the sunset, go for a swim, or simply savor the tranquility of the sea.

Exploring Manarola

Manarola is a compact village, making it easy to explore on foot. The following are some of the must-visit attractions and experiences in Manarola:

Lover's Lane (Via dell'Amore):

This famous coastal path connects Manarola to Riomaggiore and is renowned for its stunning vistas. The path is an easy hike suitable for all levels of fitness and offers romantic viewpoints ideal for watching the sunset.

The Marina and Swimming:

Manarola's small harbor is perfect for swimming and sunbathing. Crystal-clear waters and a peaceful atmosphere make it an ideal spot for a relaxing day by the sea.

Wine Tasting:

Manarola is known for producing Sciacchetrà, a sweet wine that pairs perfectly with local pastries. Visit one of the town's enotecas to sample this regional delicacy and learn about the winemaking process.

Local Cuisine:

Delight in Ligurian cuisine at Manarola's traditional trattorias and restaurants. Fresh seafood, homemade pasta, and pesto-based dishes are local specialties. Try the anchovies, which are renowned in the region.

Doria Castle:

While the castle itself is not open to the public, it offers a fantastic vantage point for panoramic views of Manarola and the surrounding area. The climb up is well worth the stunning vistas.

Church of San Lorenzo:

This Gothic church is an architectural gem. Explore its interior and admire the beautiful artwork, including a crucifix carved from a meteorite.

Festivals and Events:

Manarola hosts various festivals throughout the year, celebrating the local culture, traditions, and culinary delights. The Nativity Scene in Manarola, with its intricate and creative design, is particularly famous during the Christmas season.

Practical Information

- Accommodation: Manarola offers a range of accommodation options, including hotels, guesthouses, and vacation rentals. Booking in advance is recommended, especially during the peak tourist season.
- Transport: The Cinque Terre Card offers unlimited train travel between the five villages, including Manarola. It also provides access to the hiking trails. Consider purchasing this card for convenience.
- Language: While Italian is the official language, English is widely spoken in tourist areas.
- Safety: Manarola is a safe destination, but it's always wise to take typical precautions when traveling, such as safeguarding your belongings.
- Travel Tips: Manarola can get crowded during the day, so consider arriving early or exploring the town in the evening when it's quieter.

3.6 Riomaggiore

Nestled on the rugged cliffs of the Italian Riviera, Riomaggiore is the southernmost jewel of Cinque Terre, a UNESCO World Heritage Site. With its pastel-hued buildings, dramatic seascapes, and authentic charm, this picturesque village beckons travelers seeking an enchanting escape along the Ligurian coast.

Getting to Riomaggiore

- By Train: Riomaggiore is easily accessible by train, making it a convenient starting point for exploring Cinque Terre. The village is well-connected to major cities like Florence, Genoa, and Pisa via the regional train network.
- By Car: While cars are not allowed within Cinque Terre, you can park in La Spezia and take a short train ride to Riomaggiore. Alternatively, there are parking facilities just outside the village.

Exploring Riomaggiore

Stroll along Via Colombo:

This main street is the heart of Riomaggiore, lined with charming shops, inviting cafes, and small restaurants. It's the perfect place for a leisurely walk, absorbing the local atmosphere.

Marina and Harbor:

Riomaggiore's harbor is a bustling hub of activity. Watch as fishing boats sway gently on the water, and take in the spectacular views of the colorful buildings rising from the sea.

Church of San Giovanni Battista:

This 14th-century church, perched on a promontory, offers sweeping views of the village and the coast. The interior is adorned with beautiful frescoes and a peaceful ambiance.

Doria Castle:

A short climb from the main street leads to the historic Doria Castle. Although in ruins, it provides a spectacular vantage point for capturing the beauty of Riomaggiore and the surrounding landscape.

Via dell'Amore:

This famous lover's lane is a scenic pathway that connects Riomaggiore to Manarola. Carved into the cliffs, it offers breathtaking views of the sea and is a popular spot for romantic sunset strolls.

Local Wineries:

Riomaggiore is part of the Cinque Terre wine region, known for its unique terraced vineyards. Visit a local winery to taste the region's renowned white wine, Sciacchetrà, and learn about the traditional winemaking process.

Cuisine and Dining

Riomaggiore boasts an array of dining options, from cozy trattorias to seafront restaurants. Be sure to try local specialties like anchovies marinated in lemon and olive oil, freshly caught seafood, and the Ligurian staple, pesto. Pair your meal with a glass of Cinque Terre wine for an authentic culinary experience.

Accommodation

While Riomaggiore offers a range of accommodation options, it's advisable to book in advance, especially during the peak tourist season. You'll find charming guesthouses, boutique hotels, and apartments with stunning sea views. Consider staying in one of the historic buildings for a truly immersive experience.

Activities and Excursions

- Riomaggiore to Manarola Hike: For avid hikers, the Via dell'Amore trail offers a moderate and incredibly scenic trek between Riomaggiore and Manarola. It's a must-do for those looking to experience the breathtaking landscape up close.
- Boat Tours and Kayaking: Explore the coastline and hidden coves on a boat tour or rent a kayak for a more adventurous perspective of the cliffs and crystalline waters.

Festivals and Events

San Giovanni Battista Festival: Celebrated on June 24th, this festival honors the patron saint of Riomaggiore with religious processions, lively parades, and a festive atmosphere that brings the community together.

Practical Tips

- Riomaggiore is a pedestrian-friendly village, so comfortable walking shoes are recommended.

- Consider purchasing a Cinque Terre Card, which provides access to hiking trails and local transportation between the villages.

3.7 Hiking Trails and Scenic Routes

The Cinque Terre National Park stands as a testament to nature's grandeur and human ingenuity, offering a network of meticulously marked hiking trails that seamlessly link the five coastal villages. Whether you're a seasoned hiker or a leisurely stroller, these paths provide an intimate connection with the landscape, unveiling vistas of the rugged coastline, lush terraced vineyards, and the sparkling expanse of the Ligurian Sea.

Trails for Every Explorer

Cinque Terre boasts an array of trails, catering to a wide range of hiking enthusiasts. For the avid trekker seeking a challenge, the Sentiero Azzurro, or Blue Path, offers a comprehensive experience, winding its way along the cliffs and providing panoramic views of the Mediterranean. This iconic trail connects all five villages, allowing hikers to immerse themselves in the diverse beauty of each settlement.

For those seeking a more leisurely excursion, there are shorter, well-maintained trails that offer equally stunning perspectives. The Via dell'Amore, a gently sloping walkway that links Riomaggiore and Manarola, is a perfect introduction to the joys of Cinque Terre hiking. Carved into the cliffs, this path grants walkers unparalleled views of the azure sea, inviting them to pause and savor the majesty of their surroundings.

A Symphony of Scenic Marvels

As you embark on these trails, you'll be treated to a symphony of natural wonders. The Ligurian Sea unfurls before you, a mesmerizing expanse of vibrant blue that stretches to meet the horizon. Seagulls dance on the gentle sea breeze, their cries harmonizing with the soothing rhythm of the waves below.

The terraced vineyards, a testament to centuries of agricultural innovation, cascade down the hillsides. These meticulously constructed tiers not only create a visually stunning landscape but also produce the renowned local wine, a labor of love that has been perfected over generations.

Guidance and Precautions

While the trails are well-marked, it's advisable to pick up a detailed trail map from the park's information centers or visitor bureaus. These resources provide valuable information about trail difficulty, estimated walking times, and recommended gear.

Given the rugged terrain, it's crucial to wear comfortable, sturdy footwear. A refillable water bottle, sunscreen, and a hat are also recommended to ensure a safe and enjoyable hiking experience. Additionally, it's wise to check the weather forecast before embarking on your journey, as some trails may be temporarily closed during inclement conditions.

Embracing the Journey

Whether you choose to embark on an ambitious day-long trek or opt for a more relaxed amble along the coast, hiking in Cinque Terre is a transformative experience. Each step allows you to become one with the natural beauty that surrounds you, a reminder of the profound connection between humanity and the earth. As you navigate these trails, take moments to pause, breathe in the salty sea air, and let the awe-inspiring scenery seep into your soul.

In Cinque Terre, hiking isn't just an activity; it's a pilgrimage through a landscape that has withstood the test of time, a journey that will leave an indelible mark on your heart. So, lace up your shoes, grab your walking stick, and set forth on an adventure that promises to be nothing short of extraordinary.

3.8 Recommended Restaurants With Their Locations

1. Monterosso al Mare:

- Ristorante Miky

Address: Via Fegina, 104, 19016 Monterosso al Mare SP

Description: Known for its seafood specialties and stunning seafront location, Ristorante Miky offers a delightful culinary experience in Monterosso.

- L'Ancora della Tortuga

Address: Via Roma, 88, 19016 Monterosso al Mare SP

Description: This charming restaurant features a diverse menu of Italian and Ligurian dishes, served in a cozy atmosphere with friendly staff.

2. Vernazza:

- Trattoria da Sandro

Address: Via Roma, 22, 19018 Vernazza SP

Description: A family-run trattoria known for its traditional Ligurian cuisine, Trattoria da Sandro offers a warm, welcoming atmosphere.

- Ristorante Belforte

Address: Via Guidoni, 42, 19018 Vernazza SP

Description: Perched on a cliff, Ristorante Belforte offers breathtaking views along with a menu of fresh seafood and regional specialties.

3. Corniglia:

- Osteria a Cantina de Mananan

Address: Via Rollandi, 122, 19018 Manarola SP

Description: This cozy osteria is known for its local wine selection and serves delicious traditional dishes in a welcoming atmosphere.

- Ristorante Cecio

Address: Via Fieschi, 211, 19018 Corniglia SP

Description: With a focus on fresh, locally-sourced ingredients, Ristorante Cecio offers a menu that highlights the flavors of the region.

4. Manarola:

- Nessun Dorma

Address: Piazza Capellini, 1, 19017 Manarola SP

Description: This popular wine bar and terrace offers panoramic views of the sea and a selection of local wines, along with light bites.

- Trattoria dal Billy

Address: Via Aldo Rollandi, 122, 19017 Manarola SP

Description: Known for its warm hospitality and traditional Ligurian dishes, Trattoria dal Billy provides a memorable dining experience.

5. Riomaggiore:

- Gli Amici della Favorita

Address: Via Colombo, 121, 19017 Riomaggiore SP

Description: This family-run restaurant offers a diverse menu, showcasing both seafood and land-based dishes, in a charming setting.

- Rio Bistrot

Address: Via San Giacomo, 46, 19017 Riomaggiore SP

Description: Rio Bistrot combines creative cuisine with a relaxed atmosphere, providing a unique dining experience in Riomaggiore.

3.9 Nightclubs and Lounges with their locations

1. Vernazza:

- Il Pirata delle Cinque Terre

Location: Via Gavino, 19018 Vernazza SP, Italy

2. Monterosso al Mare:

- La Tana del Pirata

Location: Piazza Matteotti 7, 19016 Monterosso al Mare SP, Italy

3. Manarola:

- Nessun Dorma

Location: Piazza Domenico Capellini 2, 19017 Manarola SP, Italy

4. Riomaggiore:

- Bar e Vini a Pie de Ma

Location: Via San Giacomo, 64, 19017 Riomaggiore SP, Italy

5. Corniglia:

- Pan e Vin

Location: Via Fieschi, 117, 19018 Corniglia SP, Italy

Please note that the nightlife in Cinque Terre is relatively subdued compared to larger cities, and most establishments close earlier in the evening. It's recommended to check for any updated information or seasonal variations in opening hours.

CHAPTER FOUR
GENOA - MARITIME MAJESTY

4.1 Introducing Genoa

Genoa, the capital of Liguria, stands as a testament to the indelible mark that maritime history has left on its very soul. This enchanting city, cradled by the azure embrace of the Ligurian Sea, weaves together a captivating tapestry of old-world charm and a pulsating modern vibrancy. With each step through its cobbled streets, one embarks on a journey through time, traversing the epochs of seafaring grandeur and cultural opulence.

At its heart, Genoa is a city of mariners, where the rhythmic cadence of waves has provided the backdrop to centuries of maritime exploits. The whispers of ancient sailors still echo in the harbor, where colossal vessels stand as sentinels to a legacy of exploration and trade. It's here, in the Port of Genoa, that one can feel the very pulse of the city's seafaring heart, where the boundless expanse of the sea has nurtured the aspirations and dreams of generations.

Yet, Genoa is not merely a relic of the past. It is a city that has gracefully embraced the tide of progress, evolving into a modern metropolis while retaining the echoes of its storied history. Among the narrow lanes and grand piazzas, contemporary life flows seamlessly, intertwining with the ancient roots that anchor the city. The juxtaposition of sleek boutiques and centuries-old markets, of sleek skyscrapers and weathered facades, creates a dynamic urban landscape that is both evocative and exhilarating.

The historic heart of Genoa, known as the "Centro Storico," is a living testament to the city's enduring legacy. Here, narrow alleyways wind through a labyrinth of medieval architecture, revealing hidden courtyards and majestic palazzi that whisper secrets of bygone eras. Each stone, each archway, carries the weight of centuries, inviting visitors to step back in time and immerse themselves in the rich tapestry of Genoa's past.

A visit to Genoa would be incomplete without a pilgrimage to its cultural bastions. The city's historical landmarks and museums stand as guardians of its heritage, offering a captivating narrative of its evolution. The Palazzo Ducale, with its opulent halls and frescoed chambers, resonates with the echoes of dukes and nobles who shaped the city's destiny. The Cathedral of San Lorenzo, with its intricate Gothic architecture, bears witness to centuries of devotion and artistic brilliance.

Yet, Genoa's allure extends far beyond its architectural wonders. The Aquarium of Genoa, nestled along the waterfront, beckons with a world of aquatic marvels. Here, visitors can embark on an immersive journey beneath the waves, encountering a vibrant spectrum of marine life that calls the Ligurian Sea home. It's a testament to the city's ongoing relationship with the sea, inviting both young and old to marvel at the mysteries that lie beneath the surface.

In Genoa, gastronomy is not just a culinary experience; it's a celebration of tradition, a symphony of flavors that dance on the palate. This section presents a curated selection of restaurants, trattorias, and osterias that have mastered the art of Ligurian cuisine. Each recommendation is a testament to the city's dedication to authentic flavors, where freshly caught seafood mingles with aromatic herbs and locally sourced produce.

As twilight falls, Genoa's vibrant energy transforms, casting a spell of enchantment over the city. The night beckons with a wealth of options, from chic lounges perched atop historic palazzi, offering panoramic views of the sparkling sea, to lively nightclubs where the rhythm of music entwines with the beat of the heart. This section unveils the after-dark treasures of Genoa, ensuring that every visitor can find their perfect nocturnal haven.

Beyond the city's borders lie a treasure trove of day trip possibilities, each offering a unique perspective on Liguria's diverse landscape. This section reveals the enchanting destinations that await just a short journey from Genoa. From picturesque coastal towns to serene countryside escapes and historic landmarks, each recommendation is accompanied by travel tips and transportation details, ensuring that the wonders of Liguria are within easy reach.

Genoa, with its maritime soul and cultural riches, is a city that weaves history into the fabric of daily life. It is a place where the echoes of seafaring ancestors harmonize with the pulse of a modern metropolis, inviting visitors to embark on a journey through time, and experience the magic of Liguria's capital.

4.2 Historical Landmarks and Museums

Genoa, the cradle of maritime history, boasts a legacy that spans centuries. Its storied streets and grandiose edifices bear witness to the trials and triumphs of a city that once ruled the Mediterranean waves. In this section, we delve into the heart of Genoa's historical treasures, uncovering the architectural marvels and cultural institutions that weave the tale of this enchanting city.

Palazzo Ducale: A Renaissance Jewel

Location: Piazza Matteotti, 9

Standing as a testament to Genoa's golden age of wealth and influence, the Palazzo Ducale is a masterpiece of Renaissance architecture. Once the seat of power for the Republic of Genoa, its grand halls and opulent chambers resonate with the echoes of dukes and doges who shaped the city's destiny. Visitors can wander through salons adorned with frescoes by celebrated artists, immersing themselves in the splendor of a bygone era.

Cathedral of San Lorenzo: A Gothic Marvel

Location: Piazza San Lorenzo

The Cathedral of San Lorenzo, a quintessential example of Gothic architecture, stands as a spiritual beacon in the heart of Genoa's old town. Its soaring arches and intricate stone carvings bear witness to centuries of devotion and artistic brilliance. Inside, the cathedral's nave reveals a harmonious blend of faith and artistry, with awe-inspiring chapels and the ethereal light filtering through stained glass windows.

Palazzi dei Rolli: The Noble Residences

Various Locations in the Old Town

Designated as a UNESCO World Heritage Site, the Palazzi dei Rolli are a collection of magnificent palaces that once hosted visiting dignitaries during the golden age of Genoa. These opulent residences, adorned with exquisite facades and sumptuous interiors, offer a glimpse into the grandeur and refinement of the city's elite. Some of the most notable palaces include Palazzo Rosso, Palazzo Bianco, and Palazzo Doria Tursi.

Porta Soprana: Gateway to the Past

Location: Via di Porta Soprana

As one of the few remnants of Genoa's medieval fortifications, Porta Soprana stands as a tangible link to the city's distant past. This twin-towered gateway, dating back to the 12th century, once guarded the entrance to the walled city. Today, it invites visitors to step through its arches and embark on a journey through time, offering a glimpse into the city's historic defenses.

Galata Maritime Museum: Navigating the Seas of History

Location: Calata De Mari, 1

For those enraptured by Genoa's maritime legacy, the Galata Maritime Museum is a treasure trove of nautical wonders. Housed within a striking modern building, the museum's exhibits trace the evolution of seafaring, from ancient vessels to modern shipping. A highlight is the reconstruction of a 17th-century galley, providing a vivid insight into the life of sailors during the height of Genoa's maritime prowess.

Museo di Storia Naturale Giacomo Doria: Natural Wonders

Location: Via Brigata Liguria, 9

Tucked away in a neoclassical palace, the Museo di Storia Naturale Giacomo Doria invites visitors to explore the natural world through a vast collection of specimens. From exotic taxidermy to geological wonders, this museum offers a fascinating journey through the realms of biology, geology, and anthropology, shedding light on the diverse ecosystems that shape our planet.

Museo di Sant'Agostino: Art and Architecture

Location: Piazza Sarzano

Housed within a former 13th-century convent, the Museo di Sant'Agostino is a testament to the intersection of art and history. Its collection spans centuries, featuring exquisite works of art from the Middle Ages to the Renaissance. The museum's cloister, adorned with ancient frescoes, provides a tranquil oasis in the heart of the city.

Museo del Tesoro di San Lorenzo: Ecclesiastical Splendor

Location: Via San Lorenzo, 5

Hidden within the depths of the Cathedral of San Lorenzo, the Museo del Tesoro di San Lorenzo unveils a treasury of religious artifacts and precious relics. Intricately crafted chalices, sacred vestments, and priceless jewels offer a glimpse into the opulence of Genoa's ecclesiastical heritage.

The museum's collection is a testament to the devotion and craftsmanship that defined the city's religious life.

4.3 Exploring Genoa's Old Town

Genoa's Old Town, known as the "Centro Storico," is a living testament to the city's rich and storied history. With its narrow cobblestone streets, grand palaces, and hidden courtyards, this enchanting district invites visitors on a journey through time, revealing the layers of Genoa's past that have shaped its present.

The Historic Tapestry

1. Architectural Marvels

The Centro Storico is a veritable open-air museum of architectural styles spanning centuries. From the austere beauty of Romanesque churches to the opulent facades of Renaissance palaces, each building tells a story of Genoa's evolution. Notable landmarks include the stunning San Lorenzo Cathedral, a masterpiece of Gothic architecture, and the Church of San Matteo, a testament to the city's medieval splendor.

2. Palazzi dei Rolli

A unique feature of Genoa's Old Town is the Palazzi dei Rolli, a collection of grand residences that were once used to host dignitaries during state visits. These palaces, adorned with ornate facades and sumptuous interiors, provide a glimpse into the opulent lifestyle of Genoa's nobility. Some of the most notable include Palazzo Rosso, Palazzo Bianco, and Palazzo Spinola di Pellicceria.

A Walk Through History

1. Piazza de Ferrari

At the heart of the Centro Storico lies Piazza de Ferrari, a grand square that serves as the symbolic center of Genoa. It is named after the prominent Genoese banker and politician Raffaele de Ferrari. The square is adorned with the iconic bronze fountain and surrounded by impressive buildings, including the Palazzo Ducale, which once housed the Doge's palace.

2. Via Garibaldi (Strada Nuova)

Wander down Via Garibaldi, formerly known as Strada Nuova, and step into a Renaissance time capsule. Lined with meticulously preserved palaces, this UNESCO World Heritage site offers a glimpse into the opulent lifestyle of Genoa's aristocracy during the 16th and 17th centuries. The Musei di Strada Nuova, located within some of these palaces, house an extensive collection of art and artifacts.

3. Caruggi: The Ancient Alleys

The Caruggi are the charming, labyrinthine alleyways that crisscross the Old Town. These narrow passageways wind their way through the historic district, revealing hidden corners and unexpected delights. Strolling through the Caruggi, visitors can stumble upon artisan workshops, quaint cafes, and local markets, providing an authentic taste of Genoese daily life.

Art and Culture

1. Museums and Galleries

Genoa's Old Town is a treasure trove of cultural institutions. In addition to the Musei di Strada Nuova, art enthusiasts can explore the Galleria Nazionale di Palazzo Spinola, which showcases an impressive collection of Baroque art, and the Museo di Sant'Agostino, home to a diverse array of religious art and artifacts.

2. Teatro Carlo Felice

For those with a penchant for the performing arts, a visit to the Teatro Carlo Felice is a must. This historic opera house, rebuilt after World War II, hosts a vibrant program of operas, ballets, and concerts throughout the year. The theater's elegant architecture and world-class performances provide a glimpse into Genoa's enduring cultural legacy.

Gastronomic Delights

Ancient Eateries and Trattorias

The Centro Storico is also a gastronomic haven, where traditional Genoese cuisine takes center stage. Visitors can indulge in local specialties such as pesto, focaccia, and freshly caught seafood. Time-honored trattorias and osterias offer a taste of authentic Ligurian flavors, providing a culinary journey that complements the historical exploration of the district.

Hidden Gems

1. Palazzo Doria Tursi and Christopher Columbus House

Tucked away within the Old Town is the Palazzo Doria Tursi, an architectural gem that houses the City Hall of Genoa. It also hosts the Christopher Columbus House, where the explorer is believed to have once lived. This unassuming yet historically significant site offers a glimpse into the life of one of history's most renowned navigators.

2. Church of San Donato

This lesser-known gem of Genoa's Old Town is the Church of San Donato, a marvel of Romanesque architecture. Its unassuming exterior belies the stunning interior, adorned with intricately carved stone columns and ancient frescoes. This hidden sanctuary provides a peaceful respite from the bustling streets of the district.

Navigating the Centro Storico

While exploring the Centro Storico, it's advisable to wear comfortable walking shoes, as the cobblestone streets can be uneven. Guided tours are available for those seeking a deeper understanding of the district's history and significance. Additionally, many sites offer informative placards in multiple languages to enhance the visitor experience.

4.4 The Port of Genoa and Aquarium

Genoa, a city defined by its deep-rooted maritime heritage, is a captivating destination that beckons travelers from around the world. At the heart of this seafaring city lies the Port of Genoa, a bustling harbor that stands as a testament to centuries of maritime exploits. Adjacent to it is the Aquarium of Genoa, a world-class marine park that offers visitors an unparalleled opportunity to explore the wonders of the deep. In this guide, we delve into the Port of Genoa and the Aquarium, two of the city's most iconic attractions, to provide you with a comprehensive understanding of their historical significance and the thrilling experiences they offer.

The Port of Genoa: A Gateway to History

The Port of Genoa, also known as "Porto di Genova," is one of the largest and busiest seaports in the Mediterranean. It is not merely a contemporary logistical hub but a living testament to Genoa's rich maritime history. As you step into the harbor, you are transported back in time, where the echoes of ancient sailors and merchants resonate in the sea breeze. The port has been a vital center of trade, exploration, and cultural exchange for centuries.

- Historical Significance: Genoa's maritime significance dates back to the Roman Empire, and the port played a pivotal role in the Age of Exploration. It was from this harbor that Christopher Columbus set sail on his epic voyages of discovery. The port's history is interwoven with tales of conquest, trade, and the exchange of goods, ideas, and cultures.
- Exploring the Port: Today, the Port of Genoa is a bustling metropolis within the city, comprising a network of piers, terminals, and quays. As you explore the port, you'll encounter a vibrant mix of activities. Colossal cargo ships and cruise liners share the waters with fishing boats, creating a dynamic scene that showcases the port's versatility.
- Museums and Exhibits: The port is home to several museums and exhibitions that dive into its history and significance. The Galata Maritime Museum, for instance, offers a comprehensive look at Genoa's

seafaring past, complete with meticulously reconstructed ships and maritime artifacts.

The Aquarium of Genoa: An Underwater Wonderland

Adjacent to the Port of Genoa is the city's most renowned aquatic attraction—the Aquarium of Genoa. Founded in 1992 and expanded over the years, the aquarium is a world-class marine park that aims to educate, entertain, and inspire visitors of all ages. It is a place where the wonders of the deep are brought to life through a series of captivating exhibits and interactive experiences.

- Marine Biodiversity: The Aquarium of Genoa is home to an astonishing variety of marine life, showcasing creatures from the Ligurian Sea and beyond. Visitors can explore a series of immersive exhibits that take them on a journey through different ocean ecosystems. From the enchanting world of coral reefs to the mysterious depths of the open sea, the aquarium offers a window into the remarkable biodiversity of our oceans.
- Penguins and Dolphins: One of the highlights of the aquarium is the "Cetacean Pavilion," where you can witness the grace and intelligence of dolphins in action. The aquarium is also home to a colony of charismatic penguins, and their antics never fail to delight visitors of all ages.
- Interactive Experiences: The Aquarium of Genoa goes beyond traditional exhibits. It offers hands-on experiences that allow visitors to touch starfish, interact with sea turtles, and even don a wetsuit for an

up-close encounter with marine life. These experiences provide a deeper understanding of the sea and foster a sense of appreciation for the need to conserve and protect our oceans.

Practical Information

- Location: The Port of Genoa and the Aquarium are conveniently located near the city center. The port can be explored on foot, and the aquarium is situated right on the waterfront.
- Operating Hours: Both the Port of Genoa and the Aquarium have specific operating hours, so it's advisable to check their respective websites or contact them in advance to plan your visit accordingly.
- Tickets and Admission: Tickets for the aquarium are typically available for purchase both online and on-site. You may want to consider purchasing tickets in advance, especially during peak tourist seasons, to avoid long lines.
- Accessibility: The Port of Genoa and the Aquarium are generally accessible to visitors with varying degrees of mobility. However, it's a good idea to check for specific accessibility features on their websites or contact them directly for any specific needs or inquiries.

4.5 Recommended Restaurants With Their Locations

1. Trattoria da Maria

Location: Via di Sottoripa, 21, 16124 Genova GE, Italy

Description: Nestled in the heart of the historic district, Trattoria da Maria is a beloved local gem known for its authentic Ligurian cuisine. From freshly caught seafood to delectable pesto dishes, this family-run trattoria offers a true taste of Genoa.

2. Il Marin

Location: Via Antonio Gramsci, 4, 16123 Genova GE, Italy

Description: Overlooking the picturesque Porto Antico, Il Marin combines breathtaking views with exceptional seafood. With a focus on seasonal ingredients and traditional recipes, this restaurant provides a memorable dining experience.

3. Le Rune

Location: Piazza Lavagna, 18/2r, 16123 Genova GE, Italy

Description: Tucked away in the historic center, Le Rune is known for its cozy atmosphere and delectable Ligurian specialties. Diners can savor dishes made with locally sourced ingredients, all while enjoying the intimate ambiance.

4. A' Lanterna

Location: Vico di S. Luca, 3, 16123 Genova GE, Italy

Description: A' Lanterna is a charming osteria known for its warm hospitality and traditional Genoese cuisine. From hearty pasta dishes to delectable fish platters, this restaurant offers a taste of authentic Ligurian flavors.

5. Osteria da Vittorio

Location: Via dei Giustiniani, 54, 16123 Genova GE, Italy

Description: Osteria da Vittorio is a beloved eatery known for its rustic charm and impeccable seafood. The menu showcases a variety of fresh catches prepared with a touch of creativity, making it a favorite among locals and visitors alike.

6. Antica Osteria di Vico Palla

Location: Vico Palla, 15R, 16123 Genova GE, Italy

Description: Tucked away in a charming alley, Antica Osteria di Vico Palla exudes a cozy, old-world ambiance. Guests can indulge in classic Ligurian dishes prepared with care, all while enjoying the intimate setting.

7. Trattoria Ugo

Location: Via della Maddalena, 23, 16124 Genova GE, Italy

Description: Trattoria Ugo is a family-run gem that offers a warm and inviting atmosphere. Known for its traditional Genoese fare, this trattoria serves up a range of flavorful dishes, from trofie al pesto to stuffed vegetables.

4.6 Nightclubs and Lounges with Their Locations

1. Bamboo Disco Club

Location: Via degli Usodimare, 11, 16126 Genova GE, Italy

Description: Bamboo Disco Club is a popular nightclub located near the waterfront. Known for its vibrant atmosphere and diverse music selection, it's a favorite among locals and tourists alike for a night of dancing and entertainment.

2. La Funicolare Club

Location: Salita della Madonnetta, 25/r, 16122 Genova GE, Italy

Description: Situated in the heart of the city, La Funicolare Club offers a unique nightlife experience. This club is known for its eclectic music, ranging from electronic beats to live bands, and its stunning view of Genoa from its terrace.

3. Mako Discoteque

Location: Via Casaregis, 46, 16129 Genova GE, Italy

Description: Mako Discoteque is a lively nightclub with multiple dance floors and a diverse range of music genres. Located slightly outside the city center, it draws a dynamic crowd looking for a night of energetic dancing.

4. Urban Club

Location: Via Bentaccordi, 1, 16129 Genova GE, Italy

Description: Urban Club is a popular destination for electronic music enthusiasts. With its industrial-chic decor and impressive DJ lineups, it's a go-to spot for those looking to immerse themselves in the vibrant nightlife scene of Genoa.

5, Victory Morgana Bay Club

Location: Via della Rotonda, 5, 16128 Genova GE, Italy

Description: Victory Morgana Bay Club offers a sophisticated and glamorous nightlife experience. With its stylish decor, upscale ambiance, and a mix of live music and DJ sets, it's a favorite among those seeking an elegant night out.

CHAPTER FIVE

PORTOFINO AND SANTA MARGHERITA LIGURE

5.1 Portofino: A Glamorous Retreat

Portofino, often hailed as one of the most glamorous destinations on the Italian Riviera, exudes an aura of luxury and sophistication that enchants every visitor. Nestled in a secluded cove, this once-sleepy fishing village has blossomed into a celebrity hotspot, where natural beauty seamlessly mingles with refined elegance, creating an atmosphere that is nothing short of enchanting.

The Allure of Portofino's Landscape

As you approach Portofino, the first sight that greets you is a postcard-perfect panorama of vibrantly painted buildings that line the harbor. Each pastel hue seems to tell a story, and together they create a symphony of colors that dance in the Mediterranean sunlight. The sea, awash in shades of azure and emerald, stretches out to meet the horizon, mirroring the boundless sky above. Lush green hills cradle the village, their verdant embrace completing the portrait of natural beauty that defines Portofino.

The Piazzetta: Heart of the Village

At the very center of this coastal gem lies the Piazzetta, a charming square that pulsates with life. Lined with cafes, boutique shops, and lively chatter, it serves as the beating heart of Portofino. Locals and visitors alike gather here, drawn by the magnetic pull of its ambiance. Here, you can lose yourself in leisurely people-watching, sipping espresso or aperitivo, and immersing yourself in the ebb and flow of Italian life.

Castello Brown: A Fortress with a View

Overlooking the village from its perch on the hillside, Castello Brown stands as a silent sentinel to centuries of history. This historic fortress, which has witnessed the ebb and flow of empires, now opens its doors to visitors seeking a glimpse into the past. As you ascend its ancient steps, you're rewarded with panoramic views that stretch from the rugged coastline to the distant horizon. It's a perspective that leaves an indelible mark on your memory, offering a unique vantage point to appreciate the beauty of the Ligurian coastline.

Exclusive Beaches and Secluded Coves

For those in search of serenity, Portofino's beaches are a sanctuary of tranquility. The clear waters of the Ligurian Sea beckon, inviting you to take a refreshing dip. The pebbled shores, warmed by the sun, provide the perfect spot to soak in the coastal ambiance. Whether you choose to bask in the Mediterranean sun or explore the underwater wonders through snorkeling or diving, Portofino's beaches offer a peaceful escape from the cares of the world.

Luxury Spas: A Retreat for Body and Soul

Portofino's luxury spas are sanctuaries for rejuvenation and relaxation. Nestled amidst the natural beauty of the coastal landscape, these havens offer a range of treatments and therapies designed to soothe the mind and pamper the body. From massages that incorporate local herbs and oils to facials that leave your skin glowing, a visit to one of Portofino's spas is an essential part of the experience.

5.2 Santa Margherita Ligure: Beauty on the Bay

A mere stone's throw from the glamorous allure of Portofino lies the enchanting coastal town of Santa Margherita Ligure. Tucked away in a picturesque bay, this hidden gem seems to have been plucked from the pages of an Italian fairy tale. Its atmosphere resonates with timeless beauty, where every street, every waterfront view, and every historic building feels like a cherished relic from the past. Santa Margherita Ligure is a place that beckons travelers to step back in time, to savor the simple pleasures, and to immerse themselves in a culture that is steeped in tradition and charm.

A Stroll Along the Waterfront Promenade

Santa Margherita Ligure's charm is immediately evident as you wander along the waterfront promenade. Here, the bay gently laps against the shore, and the horizon seems to stretch into eternity. Palm trees sway in the breeze, casting their elegant shadows on the sun-dappled walkways. This serene scene creates an invitation for leisurely strolls, a chance to amble along the harbor and take in the coastal ambiance.

The facades of the buildings lining the waterfront are a kaleidoscope of colors, each hue telling a unique story. These painted edifices, with their shutters thrown open to catch the sea breeze, add a vibrant and enchanting backdrop to the promenade. It's a scene that captures the essence of the Italian Riviera and evokes a sense of timeless beauty.

Cultural Treasures in Santa Margherita Ligure

While Santa Margherita Ligure is undoubtedly a feast for the eyes, it's also a town with a wealth of cultural treasures waiting to be explored. At the heart of the town lies the awe-inspiring Basilica of Santa Margherita d'Antiochia, a place of worship that dates back to the 13th century. Its intricate architecture and ornate interior are a testament to the town's deep-rooted history and artistic heritage.

One of the most delightful ways to experience the local culture is by wandering through the town's lively markets. These bustling hubs of activity are where locals and visitors come together to indulge in the freshest produce, local delicacies, and artisanal crafts. The marketplaces provide a genuine glimpse into the rhythms of daily life in Santa Margherita Ligure, with colorful stalls offering everything from ripe, sun-kissed fruits to handmade trinkets.

The Lasting Impression of Santa Margherita Ligure

Santa Margherita Ligure is a town that leaves an indelible impression on all who visit. Its blend of charm, history, and natural splendor creates an experience that transcends the ordinary. Each step you take through its cobblestone streets feels like a journey back in time, to an era where life moved at a slower pace and the beauty of simplicity was celebrated.

The town's picturesque bay, adorned with colorful buildings and a palm-fringed promenade, is an enduring image of coastal elegance. Its cultural treasures, from the historic basilica to the bustling markets, add layers of depth to the town's allure. Whether you're meandering through its streets, savoring fresh seafood in a local trattoria, or simply gazing at the tranquil bay, Santa Margherita Ligure is sure to leave a lasting impression on your heart and mind. It's a place where the charm of the Italian Riviera is felt in every breeze and seen in every smile, making it an essential stop for any traveler exploring this enchanting region.

5.3 Outdoor Activities and Waterfront Views

When it comes to experiencing the splendor of the Ligurian coast, few places rival the offerings of Portofino and Santa Margherita Ligure. Nestled along the glistening waters of the Mediterranean Sea, these charming towns beckon outdoor enthusiasts and nature lovers with a wealth of activities that showcase the region's natural beauty.

Hiking Adventures along the Sentiero Azzurro

One of the most revered activities in this coastal paradise is embarking on a hike along the famed Sentiero Azzurro, or the Blue Trail. This network of trails links the five villages of Cinque Terre, and a portion of it passes through the Portofino Regional Park. The trail offers breathtaking panoramic views of the Ligurian Sea, with the emerald-green cliffs plunging dramatically into the azure waters.

For those seeking a moderate challenge, the trail from Portofino to San Fruttuoso is a must. The path winds through fragrant Mediterranean vegetation, occasionally revealing hidden coves and secluded beaches. As the trail descends to the charming San Fruttuoso Abbey, the sight of this ancient monastery against the backdrop of the sea is nothing short of awe-inspiring.

Diving into Underwater Marvels

The crystal-clear waters surrounding Portofino and Santa Margherita Ligure are a playground for diving enthusiasts. Beneath the surface lies a vibrant world of marine life, colorful coral formations, and hidden underwater caves. Diving centers in both towns offer guided tours for divers of all levels, providing a unique opportunity to explore the depths of the Ligurian Sea.

One of the most sought-after diving spots is the Portofino Marine Protected Area, which spans over 2,000 acres. Here, divers can encounter a rich tapestry of marine species, from curious octopuses to schools of iridescent fish. The submerged Christ of the Abyss statue, located near San Fruttuoso, stands as a poignant symbol of the region's commitment to marine conservation.

Sailing and Water Sports: A Maritime Playground

The azure expanse of the Ligurian Sea beckons visitors to set sail and embark on unforgettable maritime adventures. Both Portofino and Santa Margherita Ligure offer an array of options for sailing excursions, from private yacht charters to group boat tours. Gliding along the coastline, guests are treated to unrivaled views of the rugged cliffs and quaint fishing villages.

For those seeking a more interactive experience, water sports abound. Kayaking and paddleboarding enthusiasts can explore hidden coves and secret beaches, while snorkeling provides an up-close encounter with the region's diverse marine life. Adventurous souls may even try their hand at windsurfing, harnessing the gentle sea breeze for an exhilarating ride along the waves.

Leisurely Boat Tours: Reveling in Coastal Grandeur

For a more relaxed but equally enchanting experience, leisurely boat tours offer a different perspective of the Ligurian shoreline. The coastline's dramatic cliffs and lush vegetation come into full view, providing a striking contrast to the tranquil sea below.

Guided tours often include stops at some of the area's most iconic landmarks, such as the San Fruttuoso Abbey and the Abbey of Cervara. These ancient structures, nestled against the rugged terrain, offer a glimpse into the region's rich history.

Picnicking in Paradise: Secluded Beaches and Hidden Coves

For those in search of tranquility and seclusion, Portofino and Santa Margherita Ligure boast a selection of hidden beaches and coves. Accessible via hiking trails or boat, these tucked-away gems provide a peaceful escape from the more frequented areas.

A popular choice is the Paraggi Beach, a sheltered bay framed by verdant cliffs. Here, visitors can spread a picnic blanket and savor a meal amidst the serenity of nature. Alternatively, the pebbly beach of San Fruttuoso, nestled beneath the protective gaze of the abbey, offers a serene spot to unwind and bask in the Ligurian sun.

In Portofino and Santa Margherita Ligure, the outdoors seamlessly merge with the awe-inspiring coastline, offering an array of activities that cater to every adventurer's whim. Whether you're seeking an adrenaline-pumping dive into the depths or a leisurely boat tour along the cliffs, this coastal paradise promises a memorable journey amidst nature's grandeur.

5.4 Elegant Dining and Shopping

Dining and shopping in Portofino and Santa Margherita Ligure are experiences that seamlessly blend tradition with modernity, offering visitors a delightful taste of the region's cultural and culinary richness, as well as an opportunity to acquire unique treasures to remember their visit by.

Culinary Delights by the Sea

One of the most exceptional aspects of dining in these coastal towns is the profound connection to the sea. Elegant waterfront restaurants take full advantage of their stunning locations, offering patrons the chance to savor exquisite seafood dishes while gazing out over the serene waters of the Ligurian Sea. These dining establishments source their ingredients from the daily catch, ensuring that every meal is a celebration of freshness and flavor. From succulent seafood risottos to delicate grilled fish, the seafood cuisine is a highlight that never disappoints.

The traditional dishes of Liguria are celebrated in these restaurants. Pesto, the fragrant basil-based sauce that originated in the region, is a staple of the local cuisine. It graces plates of freshly made trofie pasta, creating a symphony of flavors that encapsulates the essence of Ligurian gastronomy. Dining alfresco on terraces, while the sea breeze carries the scent of the Mediterranean herbs, is a sensory experience that's sure to leave a lasting impression.

Cafes: A Glimpse into Local Life

If you're in search of a more relaxed and intimate dining experience, the charming cafes that line the streets of these towns provide a welcoming respite. Here, you can indulge in a leisurely breakfast, a mid-afternoon espresso, or a pre-dinner aperitivo while observing the ebb and flow of local life. Sip on a cappuccino or a glass of fragrant Italian wine as you watch fishermen return with their daily haul, or simply unwind and take in the captivating views of the bustling harbors.

These cafes are not just places to savor delightful beverages; they are windows into the soul of the community. Locals and tourists come together, engaging in lively conversations and people-watching, all while surrounded by the architectural charm of the towns and the sparkling sea that provides a constant backdrop. It's in these cafes that you can truly immerse yourself in the relaxed and convivial atmosphere that is so characteristic of life in Portofino and Santa Margherita Ligure.

Shopping for Treasures

When it comes to shopping, these towns offer a delightful array of boutiques and shops, catering to a diverse range of tastes and preferences. Whether you're in search of high-end fashion, artisanal crafts, or unique souvenirs, there's a little something for everyone.

High-end Designer Boutiques: For those with a penchant for luxury shopping, Portofino and Santa Margherita Ligure boast a selection of high-end designer boutiques. Here, you can find the latest Italian and international fashion collections from renowned designers. These stores offer a curated collection of apparel, accessories, and footwear that embody the sophisticated style that has come to define the coastal elite.

Artisan Workshops: Embracing the traditions of Ligurian craftsmanship, you'll discover charming artisan workshops scattered throughout the towns. These workshops produce handcrafted jewelry, pottery, and other artisanal items. Take a moment to engage with the artisans, watch them at work, and perhaps even find that unique piece to serve as a lasting memory of your visit.

Local Markets: For a more authentic taste of local culture and a chance to acquire regional specialties, don't miss the vibrant markets. These markets are where locals and visitors converge to savor the freshest produce, artisanal cheeses, and fragrant herbs. It's also an excellent place to find local wine, olive oil, and other delicacies that encapsulate the essence of the region.

Antique and Curiosity Shops: Enthusiasts of antiques and vintage collectibles will find delight in exploring the antique shops that populate these towns. From vintage furniture to quirky curiosities, these shops offer a treasure trove of unique finds that can add character and charm to your home or make for a truly distinctive gift.

Dining and shopping in Portofino and Santa Margherita Ligure are experiences that transcend the ordinary, inviting you to partake in the rich tapestry of the region's culinary heritage and indulge in retail therapy with a distinctly Ligurian flavor. With an unparalleled connection to the sea and a fusion of tradition and modernity, these towns offer a truly memorable and immersive experience for every traveler.

5.5 Recommended Restaurant With Their Locations
Portofino:

1. Ristorante Chuflay

Address: Piazza Martiri dell'Olivetta, 5, 16034 Portofino GE, Italy

Description: Nestled in the heart of Portofino, Ristorante Chuflay offers a refined dining experience with a focus on fresh, locally sourced ingredients. Diners can savor exquisite seafood dishes while enjoying panoramic views of the picturesque harbor.

2. Da O Batti

Address: Via Roma, 153, 16034 Portofino GE, Italy

Description: Da O Batti is a charming family-run restaurant known for its warm hospitality and delectable Ligurian cuisine. Located just steps from the waterfront, it's an ideal spot to indulge in traditional dishes like trofie pasta with pesto.

Santa Margherita Ligure:

1. Trattoria da Pezzi

Address: Via Jacopo Ruffini, 2, 16038 Santa Margherita Ligure GE, Italy

Description: Situated in the heart of Santa Margherita Ligure, Trattoria da Pezzi is a beloved local gem known for its authentic Ligurian flavors. The menu showcases a variety of seafood specialties and regional delicacies.

2. Osteria Sestante

Address: Via Jacopo Ruffini, 4, 16038 Santa Margherita Ligure GE, Italy

Description: Osteria Sestante offers a cozy and inviting atmosphere, perfect for indulging in traditional Ligurian dishes. The menu features a selection of fresh seafood and homemade pasta, all prepared with care and expertise.

3. Il Baretto

Address: Via dei Devoto, 34, 16038 Santa Margherita Ligure GE, Italy

Description: Il Baretto is a charming restaurant known for its intimate setting and impeccable service. Guests can enjoy a diverse menu that includes both classic Italian dishes and innovative culinary creations, all made with locally sourced ingredients.

CHAPTER SIX

THE RIVIERA DI LEVANTE

6.1 Sestri Levante: Bay of Silence and Bay of Fables

Nestled along the captivating stretch of the Ligurian coast known as the Riviera di Levante, Sestri Levante emerges as a coastal jewel, captivating visitors with its timeless beauty and tranquil ambiance. This charming town is renowned for its two iconic bays - the Bay of Silence and the Bay of Fables, each with its own unique allure and rich cultural history.

Bay of Silence: A Tranquil Oasis

As the name suggests, the Bay of Silence is a haven of serenity, where the Ligurian Sea gently caresses the shores, offering a soothing soundtrack to the discerning traveler. The soft sands invite visitors to recline and bask in the Mediterranean sun, while the crystal-clear waters beckon for a refreshing dip.

The bay exudes an air of unhurried simplicity, making it an ideal escape for those seeking respite from the hustle and bustle of modern life. Stroll along the promenade lined with quaint cafes and boutiques, savoring the unhurried pace of life that defines Sestri Levante.

Legend has it that the Danish author Hans Christian Andersen, enraptured by the bay's serene beauty, sought inspiration here and penned his beloved fairy tale "The Little Mermaid." This ethereal connection to literature and imagination infuses the Bay of Silence with an almost otherworldly charm.

Bay of Fables: Where Myth Meets Reality

Adjacent to the Bay of Silence lies the Bay of Fables, equally enchanting and steeped in legend. It is said that this bay earned its name from a centuries-old tradition where fishermen would gather to recount tales of mythical sea creatures and fantastical adventures. These captivating narratives gave birth to the moniker "Bay of Fables."

Today, the Bay of Fables invites visitors to step into a world where reality and myth converge. The waters, kissed by the golden hues of the setting sun, seem to hold the secrets of ancient mariners and storytellers. The bay's pebbled beach and surrounding cliffs provide an intimate setting for contemplation, a space where one can imagine the tales that have echoed through the ages.

Beyond the Bays: Exploring Sestri Levante

While the bays serve as the focal point of Sestri Levante's allure, the town itself boasts a wealth of cultural and historical treasures. The historic town center, characterized by pastel-hued buildings and narrow cobbled streets, invites exploration. Discover charming cafes and artisan shops, where local craftsmanship and culinary traditions thrive.

For those with an adventurous spirit, nearby hiking trails lead to panoramic viewpoints, rewarding trekkers with sweeping vistas of the Ligurian coast. The nearby hills are adorned with vineyards and olive groves, offering a taste of the region's rich agricultural heritage.

6.2 Levanto: Gateway to the Cinque Terre

Levanto, a hidden gem nestled along the Ligurian coastline, stands as the perfect gateway to the renowned Cinque Terre, a UNESCO World Heritage Site celebrated for its unparalleled beauty and charm. Unlike its more crowded neighbors, Levanto exudes a laid-back atmosphere, inviting travelers to embrace a slower pace while basking in the glory of its long sandy beach and vibrant town center. This guide will take you on a comprehensive journey through Levanto, highlighting its unique attributes and its pivotal role in accessing the Cinque Terre.

Levanto: A Hidden Gem on the Ligurian Coast

As you step into Levanto, you'll instantly notice that it exudes a distinctive charm that sets it apart from the bustling towns of the Cinque Terre. The town welcomes visitors with open arms, offering a serene and authentic coastal experience. The first point of interest that often captures the hearts of travelers is Levanto's pristine sandy beach. Unlike the pebble-lined shores of the Cinque Terre, Levanto's beach provides a comfortable and inviting place to relax and soak up the Mediterranean sun. The gentle waves beckon you to take a refreshing dip in the crystal-clear waters.

Levanto's Laid-Back Atmosphere

Levanto's allure lies in its unhurried way of life. Here, time seems to slow down, and the tranquility of the seaside envelops you, making it an ideal destination for those seeking to escape the fast pace of modern life. The town's authenticity and authenticity invite visitors to experience the true essence of the Italian Riviera. Whether you're traveling with family, friends, or on a solo adventure, Levanto provides a warm and inviting atmosphere that makes you feel at home.

Levanto's Historic Center

The heart of Levanto lies in its historic center, a labyrinth of narrow cobblestone streets that wind their way through a tapestry of colorful buildings. As you meander through these charming alleyways, you'll discover inviting piazzas where locals gather, tiny local shops offering handmade crafts and souvenirs, and charming cafes where you can sip a cappuccino or savor a gelato. One of the centerpieces of the historic district is the Church of Saint Andrew (Chiesa di Sant'Andrea) with its striking black and white striped facade. It stands as a testament to the town's rich history and cultural significance.

Outdoor Activities Abound

Levanto is not just about beachfront relaxation. It offers a range of outdoor activities for the adventurous traveler. Rent a bicycle and explore the town and its surroundings on two wheels. The gentle terrain of Levanto and the scenic routes in the vicinity make it an excellent place for cycling enthusiasts. You'll have the opportunity to traverse the coastline or venture into the lush Ligurian hills, taking in the magnificent landscapes.

Surfing and Watersports

Levanto's waters are renowned among surfers and windsurfers for their excellent conditions. The combination of reliable waves and a steady wind make it a surfer's paradise. If you're new to these water sports or wish to refine your skills, Levanto offers several local schools that provide lessons and equipment rental. The thrill of catching waves against the backdrop of the Ligurian coast is an experience that will stay with you forever.

Levanto Castle: A Glimpse into History

One of Levanto's most significant historical sites is the Levanto Castle (Castello di Levanto). Perched on a hill overlooking the town, this ancient fortress dates back to the 12th century. The castle's imposing presence is a reminder of the town's rich history, and it offers panoramic views of Levanto and its surroundings. Exploring the castle is a journey back in time, allowing you to envision the area's past and its historical significance.

Culinary Delights of Levanto

As with many towns along the Ligurian coast, Levanto takes its culinary offerings seriously. The local cuisine features a delectable array of seafood dishes, homemade pesto, and other regional specialties. Traditional trattorias and family-run restaurants line the streets, where you can indulge in mouthwatering dishes paired with local wines. Don't miss the opportunity to savor the famous trofie pasta with pesto, a Ligurian classic that tantalizes the taste buds with its simplicity and flavor.

Levanto and the Cinque Terre Connection

One of Levanto's most significant attributes is its strategic location, acting as the gateway to the Cinque Terre. This proximity to the Cinque Terre is a major advantage, as it allows travelers to explore the renowned villages with ease and convenience. Unlike the more crowded villages of the Cinque Terre, Levanto provides a tranquil and authentic experience, serving as an excellent base for your explorations.

Accessing the Cinque Terre from Levanto

From Levanto, you have several options for accessing the Cinque Terre. The most popular and convenient method is by train. The train journey offers a breathtaking coastal experience, providing passengers with stunning vistas of the rugged cliffs and azure waters that characterize the Ligurian coast. You'll find yourself gazing out the window, captivated by the mesmerizing beauty of this stretch of coastline.

Alternatively, if you're seeking a more immersive adventure and are physically fit, consider hiking along the Sentiero Azzurro, also known as the Blue Trail. This trail connects the five villages of the Cinque Terre and offers you a firsthand experience of the region's dramatic beauty. The Sentiero Azzurro meanders along the cliffs, providing unrivaled panoramic views of the sea, the villages, and the lush terraced vineyards that dot the landscape. The hike allows you to immerse yourself in the pristine natural beauty and the unique charm of each of the Cinque Terre villages.

Levanto's Advantage: A Quieter Alternative

Levanto's unique blend of tranquility and accessibility makes it the perfect choice for travelers who want to explore the Cinque Terre without the crowds. After a day of adventure in the Cinque Terre, returning to the peaceful haven of Levanto is a welcome relief. You can unwind on the beach, savor the local cuisine, or explore the town at your leisure.

Additional Benefits of Staying in Levanto

In addition to its proximity to the Cinque Terre, Levanto offers several advantages to travelers. Its strategic location on the Italian Riviera provides easy access to other remarkable destinations in the region. Day trips to nearby attractions, such as Portovenere, Porto Venere, and the Portofino Natural Park, can be easily arranged. These excursions allow you to explore the diverse landscapes and unique cultural experiences that the Ligurian coast has to offer.

Festivals and Events

Levanto hosts a variety of cultural and culinary events throughout the year, celebrating local traditions and the flavors of Ligurian cuisine. These festivals provide an opportunity to immerse yourself in the town's vibrant culture. Consider planning your visit to coincide with one of these festivities for an authentic and immersive experience.

6.3 Bonassola and Framura: Tranquil Retreats

For those who dream of a quieter escape, away from the hustle and bustle of popular tourist destinations, the adjacent villages of Bonassola and Framura beckon with their serene beauty and genuine authenticity. These hidden gems along the Ligurian coast offer a peaceful alternative to the more crowded and touristy spots, providing a more secluded, immersive experience of this picturesque region.

Bonassola: A Seaside Sanctuary

Nestled between the rugged cliffs and the Ligurian Sea, Bonassola welcomes travelers with open arms and a sense of serenity that's hard to find in more frequented coastal towns. It's a place where time seems to slow down, and the worries of the world fade away. The village's natural charm and unspoiled beauty make it a haven for those seeking tranquility.

One of the defining features of Bonassola is its enchanting beach, known as the "Spiaggia di Bonassola." This crescent-shaped stretch of shoreline is framed by soaring cliffs on one side and a lush, green hillside on the other. As you step onto the soft sands and look out at the endless blue of the Ligurian Sea, you can't help but be captivated by the stunning contrast of rugged rock formations and the gentle lap of the waves.

Sunbathing, swimming, and simply reveling in the embrace of the Mediterranean sun are all on the agenda here. For those seeking a bit of adventure, there are several options for exploration. You can take leisurely strolls along the scenic promenade, where the scent of the sea mingles with that of the nearby pine trees. The combination of salty sea air and fragrant pines creates a sensory experience that's truly invigorating.

If you're a nature enthusiast or a hiking aficionado, Bonassola has a pleasant surprise in store. The surrounding countryside offers numerous hiking trails that lead you into the heart of Liguria's natural beauty. The trails crisscross through the hills and offer panoramic views of the coastline, showcasing the harmonious blend of land and sea.

In this tranquil village, the pace of life is unhurried, and you'll soon find yourself falling into the rhythm of the locals. The heart of the village is a warm and welcoming community, with its modest but inviting local trattorias and family-run shops. Here, you can sample the authentic flavors of Liguria, with regional specialties like "trofie al pesto" and freshly caught seafood gracing your plate. Accompany your meal with a crisp glass of local wine, and you'll truly savor the Ligurian culinary experience.

Framura: A Tapestry of Hamlets

Just a stone's throw away from Bonassola lies Framura, a collection of small hamlets nestled atop the cliffs overlooking the Ligurian Sea. Framura's unique and fragmented layout adds to its charm and allure. The hamlets of Anzo, Ravecca, Setta, Costa, and Castagnola each have their own distinct character, providing a tapestry of experiences that reflect the multifaceted nature of the region.

Framura's historic core is a labyrinth of narrow alleyways that meander through ancient stone houses. These buildings, with their weathered facades and time-worn character, exude a timeless charm. As you explore the alleys, you'll be immersed in a world that seems untouched by time, where traditional Ligurian life continues as it has for centuries.

As you wander through these delightful hamlets, you may stumble upon hidden chapels, each with its own story and artistic treasures. The fragrant scent of lemon blossoms fills the air as you traverse ancient staircases, lending a sense of authenticity and charm to your exploration.

For those who appreciate the great outdoors, Framura offers a delightful network of hiking trails. These paths, once ancient mule tracks, now guide you through olive groves and vineyards, providing a firsthand encounter with the region's agricultural traditions. Whether you're a casual hiker or an avid trekker, the trails of Framura promise a journey that leads to breathtaking vistas of the Mediterranean coastline. The reward for your efforts is the chance to soak in the mesmerizing views of the Ligurian Sea, with its shades of blue and green extending as far as the eye can see.

Framura's slow pace of life and rustic authenticity make it an ideal retreat for those who appreciate the art of relaxation. It's a place where you can disconnect from the digital world and immerse yourself in the simplicity of Ligurian living.

The Magic of Tranquility

What truly sets Bonassola and Framura apart is their commitment to preserving the authentic essence of the Ligurian coast. These tranquil retreats have resisted the temptation to overdevelop and have maintained the pristine beauty of the land and the simplicity of the local way of life. Away from the clamor of larger tourist hubs, these two villages offer an opportunity to unwind, connect with nature, and savor the unhurried pace of life.

In the embrace of the Ligurian coast, Bonassola and Framura stand as a testament to the enduring allure of simplicity and natural beauty. They invite you to take a step back in time, to explore without the rush, and to relish the art of tranquility.

These are not places where you merely visit; they're places where you experience and truly live in the moment, creating memories that linger in your heart long after you've departed.

So, if you're in search of a more secluded, authentic, and tranquil retreat on the Ligurian coast, look no further than the charming villages of Bonassola and Framura. Here, you'll discover a world that moves at its own pace, where the land meets the sea in perfect harmony, and where the Ligurian way of life is an art form to be savored and remembered.

6.4 La Spezia: Gateway to the Gulf of Poets

La Spezia, often referred to as the "Gateway to the Gulf of Poets," is a vibrant and historic port city that stands as a testament to the rich maritime heritage of the Ligurian coast. While its industrial aspect may be the first impression for some, beneath this facade lies a city brimming with cultural riches, waiting to be explored and appreciated.

The heart of La Spezia boasts a historic center that exudes a distinctive charm. As you wander through its labyrinthine streets, you'll be greeted by a symphony of colors, courtesy of the quaint and vibrant facades that line the avenues. Charming squares provide spaces for locals and visitors alike to gather, chat, and soak in the atmosphere. These squares, adorned with fountains and shaded by trees, offer a moment of respite in the bustling urban landscape.

One of the highlights of La Spezia is its lively street market, where the spirit of the city truly comes alive. Here, vendors display an array of goods, from fresh produce to artisanal crafts, creating a sensory experience that immerses you in the daily life of the community. The market's bustling energy and kaleidoscope of scents, sounds, and colors provide a vibrant snapshot of Ligurian culture.

However, to truly understand the soul of La Spezia, one must venture beyond the city limits and explore the Gulf of Poets, an enchanting sanctuary that has captured the hearts and inspired the minds of poets and artists for centuries. This serene gulf, with its ethereal beauty, has been a source of solace and inspiration for some of the world's most renowned literary figures.

The Gulf of Poets owes its name to the numerous poets who sought refuge in its tranquility, finding inspiration in its idyllic surroundings. Among them, Lord Byron and Percy Bysshe Shelley stand as luminaries who sought solace along these shores. The interplay of the sea, the craggy cliffs, and the verdant landscapes creates a tapestry of natural beauty that has a timeless quality, a scene unchanged over the centuries.

As you stand at the edge of the Gulf of Poets, gazing out at the calm waters and feeling the gentle sea breeze on your skin, you can't help but be moved by the same sights and sensations that stirred the creative genius of these great poets. The Gulf whispers its secrets to those who listen, inviting you to become part of the tapestry of inspiration that has woven itself through the ages.

A visit to the Gulf of Poets is a journey not only through space but also through time, allowing you to connect with the spirits of those who, centuries ago, sought solace and creativity in this very place. It's a reminder that the natural world has the power to inspire, to heal, and to ignite the flames of imagination.

In La Spezia and the Gulf of Poets, history, culture, and nature converge in a harmonious symphony, inviting you to be a part of this timeless narrative. It's an experience that transcends the ordinary, leaving an indelible mark on your soul and a deeper appreciation for the profound beauty that lies within the heart of Liguria

CHAPTER SEVEN

THE RIVIERA DI PONENTE

7.1 Varigotti and Noli: Charming Coastal Villages

Varigotti: Where Time Stands Still

Nestled along the Ligurian Riviera, Varigotti emerges as a tranquil oasis, offering respite from the frenetic pace of larger coastal towns. Its streets, narrow and cobbled, wind their way through a tapestry of pastel-hued houses that seem plucked from a storybook. This charming village exudes an old-world charm, a place where time appears to stand still.

At the heart of Varigotti's allure stands the magnificent Saracen Tower, an ancient sentinel guarding the crystalline waters of the Ligurian Sea. This historic structure, with its weathered stone walls, is a testament to the village's rich maritime history. Ascending its timeworn steps, visitors are rewarded with sweeping vistas of the azure expanse, where sea and sky merge in an endless embrace.

Beyond the tower, Varigotti reveals another facet of its enchantment - the timeless embrace of olive groves. These ancient trees, their silvery leaves rustling in the gentle sea breeze, bear witness to centuries gone by. Wander through their midst, tracing the footsteps of generations past, and feel a profound connection to the land.

In the heart of Varigotti, the quaint church of San Lorenzo beckons with its rustic allure. This centuries-old sanctuary, with its weathered façade and ornate wooden doors, offers a sanctuary of quiet reflection. Inside, shafts of golden light filter through stained glass, illuminating a sacred space steeped in history.

Yet, perhaps Varigotti's most precious treasure lies in its shores. Pristine and inviting, the beaches of Varigotti are a sanctuary of their own. The soft, golden sands invite weary feet to sink into their warmth, while the gentle lapping of waves provides a soothing lullaby. Here, time seems to lose its urgency, and the worries of the world are swept away with each gentle tide.

Noli: The Pearl of the Riviera

Noli, often whispered as the "Pearl of the Riviera," holds court on the Ligurian coastline with an undeniable grace. Steeped in maritime heritage, this village breathes life into the stories of sailors, traders, and explorers of days gone by. Its medieval heart beats with a rhythm that resonates through the cobblestone streets.

Dominating the skyline, the Castello di Monte Ursino stands as both sentinel and storyteller. This ancient fortress, with its weathered stone walls and crenellated towers, offers a vantage point like no other. From its lofty heights, the expanse of the Ligurian Sea unfolds in all its splendor, a testament to the enduring allure of the maritime world.

The sea, a constant companion, whispers tales of adventure and discovery to those who stroll along Noli's seafront promenade. Here, the scent of salt mingles with the melodies of fishermen as they mend their nets, weaving a tapestry of traditions that echo through the ages. The promenade, lined with cafes and boutiques, offers a delightful interlude for those seeking to soak in the atmosphere.

Yet, it is within Noli's historic center that the true essence of the village comes to life. The narrow alleyways, adorned with climbing bougainvillea and ancient stones, invite exploration. At every turn, glimpses of a storied past emerge - a centuries-old fountain, a weathered plaque, a facade bearing the scars of time. Here, history is not confined to books; it is woven into the very fabric of the village.

As day turns to dusk, Noli's trattorias come to life, offering a symphony of flavors for the discerning palate. Delectable seafood dishes take center stage, each bite a tribute to the bounties of the sea. The catch of the day, lovingly prepared with a blend of traditional techniques and modern creativity, invites diners on a culinary journey that mirrors Noli's own legacy of exploration and innovation.

7.2 Albenga: Ancient Wonders and Culinary Delights

As you step onto the cobbled streets of Albenga, you're transported to an era long past, where history whispers from every stone. This ancient city is a living testament to Liguria's rich and layered past. Its very foundations are steeped in stories, and its alleys echo with the footfalls of generations.

The beating heart of Albenga lies within its remarkably preserved Roman quarter. Here, one can't help but stand in awe of the remnants of the once-mighty Roman city. The imposing city walls, their ancient stones bearing the weight of centuries, stand as silent sentinels to a time of grandeur.

The bridges, though weathered, still evoke the engineering marvels of their creators. And then, there's the amphitheater, a testament to the gatherings and spectacles that once defined daily life in ancient Albenga.

Wandering deeper into the heart of Albenga, the Old Town beckons with its labyrinthine alleys and historic churches. Each turn presents a new vista, a hidden courtyard, or a glimpse of a bygone era. The ancient stones seem to murmur secrets of days long gone, inviting you to lose yourself in their tales.

One cannot speak of Albenga without mentioning the iconic Church of San Michele. Its presence is commanding, its bell tower reaching for the heavens. As you stand before it, you're met with a sense of reverence, a feeling that you're in the presence of something truly special. Step inside, and you're greeted by a sanctuary adorned with intricate frescoes, each brushstroke a testament to the artistry of ages past.

After a day of absorbing the rich tapestry of Albenga's history, it's time to indulge in its culinary treasures. Albenga is known for its culinary prowess, and the streets are lined with eateries eager to showcase their specialties. The renowned Focaccia di Recco is a must-try, a delicate dance of thin, crispy dough enveloping creamy stracchino cheese. It's a flavor explosion that lingers on the palate, a taste of Ligurian culinary genius.

Seafood takes center stage in Albenga's gastronomic repertoire, and rightly so. The catch of the day, plucked fresh from the Ligurian Sea, graces the tables of local restaurants. Each dish is a celebration of the sea's bounty, prepared with a reverence for tradition and a flair for innovation. From delicate crudo to hearty seafood stews, Albenga's culinary offerings are a testament to the region's close relationship with the sea.

In Albenga, time seems to flow at its own unhurried pace. It's a city where history isn't confined to museums and books, but lives and breathes in every corner. As you meander through its streets, you're not just a visitor; you're a traveler through time, a witness to the ebb and flow of centuries. Albenga welcomes you to step back in time, and in doing so, invites you to be a part of its enduring story.

7.3 Imperia: Olive Oil Capital of Italy

Nestled at the confluence of majestic mountains and the azure expanse of the Ligurian Sea, Imperia stands as a testament to Liguria's rich cultural and culinary heritage. This city is more than a mere destination; it's a living, breathing chronicle of a region deeply entwined with the land and sea.

Olive oil is not just a commodity in Imperia; it's a way of life. The hillsides that cradle the city are adorned with ancient olive groves, their gnarled trunks and silvery leaves whispering secrets of centuries gone by. It is from these venerable trees that some of Italy's finest olive oils are born, their flavors a reflection of the sun-drenched terroir of Liguria.

For those eager to delve into the art and tradition of olive oil production, the Olive Oil Museum beckons. Here, amid the fragrance of freshly pressed olives and the hum of ancient machinery, visitors gain a profound understanding of the age-old techniques that have shaped Imperia's identity. It's a journey through time, a glimpse into the toil and dedication that goes into each precious drop of liquid gold.

Wandering through the Parasio, Imperia's historic district, is akin to stepping into a medieval tableau. The narrow, winding streets, lined with weathered stone buildings, exude a timeless charm. Each corner reveals a new discovery - a hidden courtyard, a centuries-old fountain, or an artisan's workshop. Here, the echoes of history reverberate, inviting you to trace the footsteps of those who walked these streets long ago.

Imperia's markets are a sensory feast, a celebration of the region's bountiful harvests. The stalls burst with vibrant colors - plump tomatoes, fragrant basil, and the jewel-like hues of freshly picked fruits. Among these treasures, the Taggiasca olives reign supreme. Renowned for their delicate flavor and buttery texture, they are a coveted ingredient in Ligurian cuisine. To sample these olives is to taste the essence of Imperia itself.

While steeped in tradition and heritage, Imperia is not confined to its historic roots. It also boasts a coastline graced with beautiful beaches, offering a perfect blend of cultural enrichment and seaside relaxation. The sun-drenched shores invite leisurely strolls along the water's edge, while the gentle lapping of waves provides a soothing soundtrack to the day.

In Imperia, the past and present intertwine seamlessly, creating a tapestry of experiences that linger in the memory. It's a city where the rhythms of life are attuned to the land and sea, where every olive tree and sea breeze carries a piece of history. Imperia extends an invitation to immerse yourself in its stories, to savor its flavors, and to become a part of its enduring narrative.

CHAPTER EIGHT

THE HINTERLAND - MOUNTAINS AND OLIVE GROVES

8.1 The Ligurian Alps: Nature's Playground

Nestled in the northernmost corner of Liguria, the Ligurian Alps offer a breathtaking contrast to the coastal landscapes. Towering peaks, lush valleys, and pristine lakes make this region a haven for nature enthusiasts. The Parco Naturale Regionale delle Alpi Liguri, a regional natural park, encompasses much of this area, providing a protected environment for a diverse range of flora and fauna.

A Symphony of Nature's Wonders

The Ligurian Alps unfold like a majestic symphony, with each note composed of dramatic peaks and sweeping valleys. Here, the mountains reach for the sky, their rugged profiles etched against the horizon. Verdant valleys cradle picturesque hamlets, while alpine lakes mirror the azure heavens above. This is a realm of unspoiled beauty, where nature reigns supreme, inviting explorers to embark on an unforgettable journey.

Activities in the Ligurian Alps

1. Hiking and Trekking:

The Ligurian Alps boast an extensive network of trails that meander through alpine meadows, offering hikers an intimate encounter with nature's grandeur. From leisurely strolls to challenging ascents, there's a path to suit every level of adventurer. As you traverse these trails, the air becomes crisp and invigorating, and with every step, the landscape unfurls in ever more captivating vistas. The scent of pine mingles with wildflowers, creating an olfactory tapestry that complements the visual feast.

2. Mountain Biking:

For the intrepid cyclist, the Ligurian Alps present a thrilling challenge. The rugged terrain, with its undulating slopes and exhilarating descents, promises an adrenaline-pumping ride. Trails wind through forests and over rocky outcrops, offering a rollercoaster experience for those on two wheels. Whether you're a seasoned mountain biker or a novice looking for adventure, the Ligurian Alps deliver an unforgettable ride.

3. Wildlife Watching:

As you navigate the trails of the Ligurian Alps, keep a keen eye out for the local fauna that call this region home. Among the craggy rocks, you may spot the sure-footed chamois, a symbol of the Alps' untamed spirit. Majestic ibex may make a cameo, their impressive antlers silhouetted against the skyline. Above, a variety of bird species grace the skies, their graceful flight adding an ethereal quality to the landscape.

Noteworthy Sites

1. Colle di Tenda:

This historic mountain pass stands as a testament to the enduring ties between Liguria and France. It was here that traders, travelers, and armies traversed the rugged terrain, leaving their mark on the landscape and the annals of history. As you stand at Colle di Tenda, you'll be transported back in time, with the sweeping views reminding you of the strategic importance this pass held in ages past.

2. Lakes of the Ligurian Alps:

Lago di Négozio and Lago delle Lame, nestled within the heart of the Ligurian Alps, offer tranquil oases amid the dramatic terrain. These crystalline lakes mirror the surrounding peaks, creating a serene tableau of nature's artistry. Whether you choose to simply bask in the stillness or partake in a leisurely lakeside picnic, these spots provide a respite from the rigors of exploration.

In the Ligurian Alps, nature's grandeur knows no bounds. Each step unveils a new wonder, each vista leaves an indelible impression. This is a place where the soul finds solace in the embrace of the mountains, and where every corner reveals a new facet of the natural world. It's an invitation to not only explore, but to become a part of the symphony of the Ligurian Alps.

8.2 Dolceacqua and Apricale: Medieval Magic

Tucked away in the hills of Liguria, Dolceacqua and Apricale are two charming medieval villages that seem frozen in time. Cobbled streets, stone buildings, and ancient bridges lend an air of enchantment to these settlements. As you wander through their narrow alleys, it's easy to imagine yourself stepping back into a bygone era, where the pace of life was unhurried, and history whispered from every corner.

Dolceacqua: A Timeless Haven

Dolceacqua, cradled along the banks of the Nervia River, is a testament to the enduring allure of medieval architecture. Here, time seems to stand still, allowing visitors to immerse themselves in the rich tapestry of history.

1. The Doria Castle:

Perched strategically on a hill overlooking the village, the Doria Castle stands as a sentinel, offering panoramic views that stretch as far as the eye can see. This well-preserved fortress, built in the 12th century, bears witness to the village's storied past. As you ascend its stone steps and pass through its ancient gates, you'll be transported to a time when knights roamed the land and battles shaped the destiny of these hills.

2. Monet's Bridge:

The "Ponte Vecchio," an iconic stone bridge immortalized by Claude Monet in his 1884 painting, is a testament to the timeless beauty of Dolceacqua. This arching span, with its humpbacked silhouette, stretches gracefully across the Nervia River. Here, artists and photographers find inspiration in the interplay of light and shadow, capturing the essence of Dolceacqua's enchantment. As you stroll across its ancient stones, you'll feel a connection to the artists who came before, seeking to capture the essence of this idyllic setting.

Apricale: A Medieval Gem

High atop a hill, Apricale commands a view of the surrounding countryside that is nothing short of breathtaking. This ancient village, with its labyrinthine alleys and time-worn buildings, exudes a sense of mystery and wonder.

1. The Castle of the Lizard:

Perched at the highest point of Apricale, the Castle of the Lizard stands as a sentinel, its stone walls weathered by centuries of history. From this vantage point, the vista opens up, revealing a patchwork of fields and vineyards, punctuated by distant peaks. The castle's battlements provide a glimpse into the village's medieval defenses, while its tower offers an unrivaled panorama of the Ligurian landscape. As you explore its nooks and crannies, you'll be transported to an era of knights, lords, and ancient legends.

2. Artistic Heritage:

Apricale wears its artistic heart on its sleeve. Galleries and sculptures adorn the village, each piece a testament to the enduring creative spirit that thrives here. Artists from around the world have found inspiration in Apricale's timeless beauty, capturing its essence on canvas and in stone. As you meander through the village's alleys, you'll encounter a tapestry of artistic expression, each piece adding a layer to Apricale's vibrant cultural tapestry.

In Dolceacqua and Apricale, time takes on a different meaning. It slows to a leisurely pace, allowing you to savor every stone, every cobble, every whispered tale of days long past. These villages are not simply places to visit; they are experiences that linger in the soul, inviting you to become a part of their enduring story. Here, history and enchantment intertwine, creating a tapestry that is uniquely Ligurian.

8.3 Traditional Festivals and Events

Liguria, a region steeped in history and cultural diversity, comes alive throughout the year with a vibrant tapestry of festivals and events. Each celebration offers a unique glimpse into the heart of Ligurian culture, providing visitors with an opportunity to immerse themselves in centuries-old traditions and revel in the lively spirit of the locals.

Noteworthy Festivals:

1. La Festa della Stella Maris (Feast of the Sea):

In various coastal towns along Liguria's picturesque shoreline, the sea is not just a backdrop, but a vital part of life itself. This sentiment is beautifully captured in the La Festa della Stella Maris, an event that pays homage to Liguria's deep connection with the vast Mediterranean. The festivities unfold with processions, where fishermen and locals parade through the streets, bearing symbols of their maritime heritage. The air is filled with the aromas of freshly cooked seafood, enticing visitors to indulge in sumptuous feasts prepared with the day's catch. Boat parades grace the sparkling waters, their colorful sails billowing in the breeze, creating a spectacle that is both awe-inspiring and deeply moving. As the sun dips below the horizon, casting its warm hues across the sea, the Feast of the Sea culminates in a display of fireworks that light up the night sky, symbolizing the enduring bond between Ligurians and their beloved sea.

2. Infiorata:

In towns such as Noli and Ventimiglia, the arrival of spring heralds a transformation that is nothing short of enchanting. Streets that once echoed with footsteps now burst forth in a riot of color and fragrance as the Infiorata takes center stage. This floral festival is a testament to Liguria's love affair with nature's beauty. Skilled artisans and passionate locals come together to create intricate tapestries of petals and blooms, adorning the cobblestones with breathtaking designs that seem to dance in the gentle breeze. Each step is a sensory delight, with the delicate perfume of flowers mingling with the lively chatter of visitors. The Infiorata is a celebration of life, a reminder of the beauty that can be found in even the simplest of moments, and a tribute to the boundless creativity that flows through Liguria's veins.

Folklore and Music:

1. Sagra degli Agrumi (Citrus Festival):

In places like Ventimiglia, where the sun-kissed hillsides yield some of the finest citrus fruits in the region, the Sagra degli Agrumi is a lively celebration of the land's bounty. This festival is a sensory explosion, where vibrant oranges, lemons, and grapefruits take center stage. The streets come alive with parades, showcasing the vibrant colors and shapes of these prized fruits. Visitors have the opportunity to explore exhibitions that delve into the history and cultivation of citrus, gaining a deeper appreciation for the artistry and dedication that goes into their cultivation. And of course, no celebration of citrus would be complete without tastings, where the tangy sweetness of Ligurian citrus fruits can be savored in a multitude of delectable forms.

2. Festa della Focaccia (Focaccia Festival):

In various towns across Liguria, the beloved flatbread known as focaccia takes on a special significance. The Festa della Focaccia is a celebration of Ligurian cuisine at its most comforting and quintessential. Locals and visitors alike gather to revel in the simple yet sublime pleasure of freshly baked focaccia. Competitions showcase the skill and creativity of bakers who vie to create the most delectable and beautifully crafted versions of this cherished staple. Tastings offer a journey through the diverse flavors and toppings that adorn focaccia across Liguria. It's a celebration of community, of sharing a meal that transcends generations, and a reminder of the deep-rooted culinary traditions that bind Ligurians together.

CHAPTER NINE
NAVIGATING LIGURIA

9.1 Transportation Options

Liguria, a region renowned for its stunning coastal landscapes and charming historic towns, presents a diverse array of transportation options tailored to meet the needs of every traveler. The well-organized transport infrastructure ensures that exploring this picturesque region is a seamless and enjoyable experience.

9.1.1 Train Networks: Navigating the Scenic Routes

Liguria, an Italian region of captivating beauty, is blessed with an enchanting coastline, charming historic towns, and an extensive train network that allows you to explore its scenic wonders with ease. The train system in Liguria is not just a mode of transportation; it's a breathtaking journey in itself. This guide provides essential information for tourists looking to explore Liguria's picturesque landscapes and historic towns via its train networks.

1. The Ligurian Train Network: An Overview

Liguria's train system is known for its efficiency and stunning routes that offer travelers the opportunity to marvel at the natural beauty of the region. The primary train operator in Liguria is Trenitalia, which connects major cities and towns, making it an ideal mode of transport for tourists. The main railway lines in Liguria include the Genoa-Rome line, the Genoa-Milan line, and the Genoa-Pisa line, which ensure easy access to some of the most iconic destinations in the region.

2. Scenic Train Routes in Liguria

One of the highlights of traveling by train in Liguria is the opportunity to witness its breathtaking scenery. Here are some of the most scenic train routes you should not miss:

- Cinque Terre Line: This line connects La Spezia to the five colorful villages of Cinque Terre (Monterosso, Vernazza, Corniglia, Manarola, and Riomaggiore). The train journey offers mesmerizing views of the Ligurian Sea, vineyard-covered hills, and picturesque coastal villages. Be sure to have your camera ready for this remarkable ride.
- Genoa to Portofino: The train from Genoa to Santa Margherita Ligure and Portofino provides stunning vistas of the Ligurian coastline. As you pass through charming seaside towns, you'll be treated to panoramic views of the Gulf of Tigullio and the crystalline waters that characterize this stretch of the Italian Riviera.
- Genoa to Ventimiglia: This coastal route offers scenic views of the Ligurian Sea as it hugs the shoreline, passing by elegant towns like Alassio, Sanremo, and Ventimiglia. The journey is a delight for those seeking to experience the beauty of the Mediterranean coast.
- Genoa to La Spezia: The journey from Genoa to La Spezia provides travelers with a glimpse of both the urban and natural wonders of Liguria. You'll pass through Genoa's historic center and eventually make

your way along the coast, witnessing captivating landscapes as you approach La Spezia.

3. Train Tickets and Reservations

Train tickets in Liguria can be purchased at train stations, online, or through ticket machines. To secure a seat on popular routes or during peak travel times, it's advisable to make reservations in advance. Tickets are available for different classes, including First Class (Prima Classe) and Second Class (Seconda Classe). First Class offers more space and comfort, while Second Class is a budget-friendly option that is perfectly comfortable for most travelers.

4. Timetables and Schedules

Train schedules can vary, so it's essential to check timetables in advance. Major stations in Liguria, such as Genoa Piazza Principe and La Spezia Centrale, have regular departures to popular destinations. Be sure to arrive at the station with enough time to purchase tickets, go through security checks, and locate your platform.

5. Navigating Train Stations

Italian train stations, including those in Liguria, are generally well-organized and equipped with clear signage in multiple languages. Station facilities typically include waiting areas, restrooms, ticket counters, and information booths. Most train stations are also accessible to travelers with disabilities.

6. Travel Tips for a Comfortable Journey

- Seat Selection: If you're looking to capture the best views, consider sitting on the side of the train that faces the coast. This way, you can take in the magnificent scenery as you journey through Liguria.
- Luggage: Travelers are allowed to bring luggage on trains, but be mindful of space limitations. Store your luggage in designated areas and keep smaller bags and valuables with you.
- Food and Refreshments: Most trains in Liguria have a dining car or offer refreshments from a trolley. However, it's a good idea to bring snacks and drinks, especially if you're on a longer journey.
- Travel Apps: Consider using travel apps to access real-time information on train schedules and routes. Apps like Trenitalia and Italo can be valuable companions during your journey.

7. Accessibility and Assistance

If you require special assistance due to disabilities or other needs, Italian train services are equipped to assist you. Contact the train company or station staff in advance to arrange for any necessary accommodations.

8. Safety and Security

While traveling by train in Liguria is generally safe, it's essential to stay alert and vigilant. Keep an eye on your belongings, especially in crowded train stations. Liguria is known for its hospitality, and locals are often willing to help travelers with information and directions.

9. Fare Discounts and Travel Cards

If you plan to use the train frequently during your stay in Liguria, consider purchasing regional travel cards or discount passes, which can offer substantial savings on train fares.

10. Conclusion

Traveling by train in Liguria is not just a means of transportation; it's a journey through some of Italy's most captivating landscapes. Whether you're exploring the dramatic coastline of Cinque Terre or the historic treasures of Genoa, the train networks in Liguria make it convenient to experience the region's wonders. Be sure to plan your journeys in advance, savor the views, and embrace the charm of Liguria from the comfort of its scenic railways.

9.1.2 Local Buses and Taxis: Navigating Urban Centers

When exploring the enchanting urban centers of Liguria, getting around efficiently is essential to make the most of your visit. This guide provides comprehensive information on utilizing local buses and taxis, ensuring you can navigate Liguria's historic towns and cities with ease.

1. Understanding the Local Bus System

Liguria boasts a well-organized and reliable network of local buses that serve the region's towns and cities. Here's what you need to know:

Routes and Stops

Local buses typically operate on established routes, connecting key points within urban centers. Stops are clearly marked, and routes are well-documented, allowing you to plan your journey effectively. Maps and schedules are available at bus stations and online, making it convenient to determine the best route for your intended destination.

Ticketing and Fares

Tickets for local buses can usually be purchased directly from the driver upon boarding. It's advisable to carry small denominations of currency for ticket purchases. Some urban centers may also offer the option of purchasing tickets in advance at designated kiosks or online platforms.

Timetables and Frequency

Buses in Liguria generally adhere to a regular schedule, with increased frequency during peak hours. Be sure to check the timetable beforehand to avoid any unnecessary waiting. For real-time updates, various smartphone apps and online resources provide live tracking of buses, ensuring you can plan your journey down to the minute.

Accessibility

Most local buses in Liguria are equipped with features to accommodate passengers with reduced mobility. These include ramps for wheelchair access and designated spaces for strollers.

2. Navigating Urban Centers by Taxi

Taxis offer a convenient and direct mode of transportation within urban centers. Here's what you need to know about using taxis in Liguria:

Hailing a Taxi

Taxis are readily available at designated taxi stands, transportation hubs, and popular tourist areas. In urban centers, you can also hail a taxi from the street if it's illuminated and has a "taxi" sign on the roof.

Fare Structure

Taxis in Liguria typically operate on a metered fare system, with rates varying based on distance traveled. There may be additional charges for luggage, late-night travel, and public holidays, so it's advisable to confirm the fare structure with the driver before beginning your journey.

Payment Methods

While cash is widely accepted, an increasing number of taxis in urban centers now offer electronic payment options, including credit and debit cards. It's recommended to confirm payment methods with the driver before embarking on your journey.

Language and Communication

While many taxi drivers in Liguria may have a basic understanding of English, it's beneficial to have your destination written down or displayed on a map to ensure clear communication.

3. Travel Tips for Local Buses and Taxis

- Plan Ahead: Familiarize yourself with the routes, schedules, and fare structures beforehand to streamline your journey.
- Have Small Change: Carry small denominations of currency to facilitate ticket purchases and taxi fares.
- Use Apps for Real-Time Information: Smartphone apps and online resources provide real-time updates on bus locations and taxi availability.
- Verify Fare: Confirm the fare with the taxi driver before starting your journey, especially for longer trips.
- Be Aware of Peak Hours: Expect increased demand for both buses and taxis during rush hours and plan accordingly.

By understanding the nuances of using local buses and taxis in Liguria's urban centers, you'll be well-equipped to navigate the region's historic towns and cities seamlessly, ensuring an enriching and enjoyable travel experience.

9.1.3 Ferry Services: Embracing Coastal Splendor

Liguria, with its rugged coastline and charming seaside towns, beckons travelers to explore its coastal splendor in a way that is both enchanting and convenient - through the region's extensive ferry services. These vessels serve as a vital link, connecting the picturesque towns that hug the Ligurian coastline. A ferry ride in Liguria is not just a mode of transportation; it's an experience that offers unparalleled views and an opportunity to immerse oneself in the natural beauty that defines this region.

Seamless Connections Across the Ligurian Sea

Ferry services in Liguria offer seamless connections between the region's most iconic coastal destinations. From the colorful villages of Cinque Terre to the glamorous shores of Portofino, these vessels traverse the Ligurian Sea, providing an alternative perspective of the coastline's stunning topography. The journey itself is a visual feast, allowing passengers to witness the dramatic cliffs, serene bays, and architectural marvels that define Liguria.

Navigating Coastal Towns

For tourists eager to explore the coastal towns, ferries offer a convenient and scenic alternative to land-based transportation. The coastal terrain of Liguria, characterized by its steep cliffs and rugged coastline, often makes access by road or rail challenging. Ferries bypass these obstacles, providing a direct route to these charming villages. Whether you're enchanted by the pastel-hued buildings of Vernazza or yearning to experience the glamour of Santa Margherita Ligure, ferries make it possible to effortlessly hop from one coastal gem to another.

Practical Information for Ferry Travel

Before embarking on a ferry journey, it's essential to be armed with some practical information:

- Schedules and Routes: Familiarize yourself with the ferry schedules and routes. These may vary depending

on the season, so it's advisable to check for updates or changes.
- Ticketing and Boarding: Tickets can be purchased at designated ticketing booths or online, depending on the ferry company. Arrive at the port with ample time to spare, especially during peak tourist seasons, to ensure a smooth boarding process.
- Luggage Considerations: While there are generally no strict luggage restrictions, it's recommended to travel light, as space on board may be limited. Larger suitcases can be stowed away, but it's wise to keep essential items in a smaller bag.
- Seating Options: Ferries typically offer a range of seating options, from standard seats to more luxurious accommodations. Consider your preferences and budget when selecting your seating.
- Weather Considerations: While ferries operate in various weather conditions, it's advisable to check the weather forecast, especially if you're prone to seasickness. In case of adverse conditions, ferry schedules may be subject to change.

Exploring Beyond the Coastline

In addition to connecting coastal towns, some ferry routes offer excursions to nearby islands or other points of interest. For instance, a ferry ride to the enchanting island of Palmaria from Portovenere offers a unique perspective of the coastline and the opportunity to explore the island's natural beauty.

Ferry services in Liguria present an extraordinary opportunity to not only traverse the Ligurian Sea but to truly embrace the coastal splendor that defines this region. The experience of sailing along this breathtaking coastline is sure to leave an indelible mark on any visitor, providing memories that will be cherished long after the journey concludes. So, set sail and let the Ligurian Sea unveil its coastal treasures in all their splendor.

9.1.4 Car Rentals: Crafting Personal Journeys

For the intrepid traveler seeking the freedom to explore Liguria on their terms, renting a car is an excellent choice. This picturesque region, with its winding coastal roads, charming hilltop villages, and hidden coves, is best experienced when you have the autonomy to meander and uncover its hidden treasures. Here's everything you need to know about car rentals in Liguria.

Choosing the Right Rental Company

When selecting a car rental agency, opt for reputable and well-established companies with positive customer reviews. Major international brands like Hertz, Avis, and Europcar have a presence in Liguria, offering a wide range of vehicle options and comprehensive services.

Booking in Advance

It's advisable to book your rental car in advance, especially during peak tourist seasons. This ensures that you have a wider selection of vehicles to choose from and helps secure the best rates. Online platforms and dedicated rental company websites are convenient booking channels.

Driver's License and Age Requirements

To rent a car in Liguria, you must possess a valid driver's license from your home country. While the minimum age for renting a car is typically 21, some agencies may have specific age restrictions or surcharges for drivers under 25. Be sure to check the rental company's policy beforehand.

Vehicle Options

Rental agencies in Liguria offer a diverse range of vehicles, from compact cars ideal for navigating narrow coastal roads to spacious SUVs for families or groups. Consider factors such as the number of passengers, luggage space, and the type of terrain you plan to cover when making your selection.

Insurance and Additional Coverage

Basic rental rates usually include collision damage waiver (CDW) and theft protection, which limit your liability in case of an accident or theft. However, it's recommended to consider additional coverage options like personal accident insurance (PAI) and supplementary liability insurance (SLI) for added peace of mind. Check with your rental company about available coverage options.

Navigating Ligurian Roads

- Road Conditions: The roads in Liguria are generally well-maintained, but you'll encounter a mix of highways, winding coastal roads, and mountainous terrain. Take note of any road signs indicating special conditions or restrictions.

- Parking: In popular tourist areas like Cinque Terre or Genoa, parking can be challenging to find, especially during peak hours. Consider using municipal parking lots or garages for a hassle-free experience.
- ZTL Zones: Some historic city centers, like Genoa's Old Town, have restricted traffic zones (ZTL). Pay attention to signage and consider parking outside these areas and using public transportation to explore them.
- Fuel: Gas stations are abundant throughout Liguria, and self-service options are available. Remember that many stations may only accept cash, so it's a good idea to have some on hand.
- Tolls: Liguria has a few toll roads, notably the Autostrada (A10) that runs along the coast. Keep some change or a credit card handy for toll payments.

Exploring Beyond the Coast

While Liguria's coastline is undoubtedly captivating, the region's inland areas hold their own treasures. Consider venturing into the Ligurian Alps or exploring the picturesque villages nestled in the hills. A rental car affords you the flexibility to uncover these lesser-known gems.

Returning the Rental Car

When returning your rental car, ensure you follow the company's guidelines for drop-off procedures. Check for any damages, refill the tank if required, and return any rental accessories like GPS devices or child seats.

9.2 Travel Safety Tips

Liguria, with its captivating coastline and historic towns, is a treasure trove for travelers seeking a taste of authentic Italy. While the region exudes charm and beauty, it's essential to prioritize safety during your visit. This guide provides valuable insights and tips to ensure a secure and enjoyable experience exploring Liguria.

1. Stay Informed and Plan Ahead

Before embarking on your Ligurian adventure, conduct thorough research on the region. Familiarize yourself with local customs, emergency contacts, and potential safety concerns. Stay updated on weather forecasts, especially if you plan on engaging in outdoor activities.

2. Choose Safe Accommodation

Opt for reputable and well-reviewed accommodations. Prioritize establishments located in safe neighborhoods and consider factors like proximity to public transportation and emergency services. Ensure your lodgings have adequate security measures in place.

3. Keep Valuables Secure

While Liguria is generally safe, it's crucial to exercise caution with your belongings. Use a secure, anti-theft bag or backpack to carry your valuables. Avoid displaying expensive jewelry or electronics, and be mindful of pickpockets in crowded areas.

4. Emergency Contacts

Familiarize yourself with essential emergency numbers in Liguria:

- Emergency Services: Dial 112 for police, medical, or fire emergencies.
- Tourist Helpline: +39 06 4967 7517 - This English-speaking helpline can assist tourists in case of non-emergency situations or provide general information.

5. Cultural Sensitivity

Respect local customs and traditions. Dress modestly when visiting religious sites, and be mindful of local norms regarding behavior and etiquette. This demonstrates cultural appreciation and enhances your overall experience.

6. Travel Insurance

Obtaining comprehensive travel insurance is crucial. Ensure your policy covers potential medical emergencies, trip cancellations, and any activities you plan to undertake in Liguria. This provides peace of mind in case of unexpected situations.

7. Be Cautious in Crowded Areas

Exercise heightened vigilance in bustling tourist spots, train stations, and markets. Keep your belongings close, and be aware of your surroundings. Avoid carrying large amounts of cash and consider using a money belt for added security.

8. Transportation Safety

- Trains and Buses: Use official and well-lit transportation hubs. Be mindful of your belongings while on board, and validate tickets before boarding.
- Taxis: Only use licensed taxis from reputable companies. Confirm the fare before starting your journey.
- Ferries: Follow safety instructions provided on board. Be cautious when embarking or disembarking.

9. Health Precautions

Ensure you have necessary vaccinations and medications before traveling to Liguria. Carry a basic first-aid kit with essentials like band-aids, pain relievers, and any prescription medications.

10. Natural Hazards

If you plan on hiking or exploring natural sites, be aware of potential risks like slippery trails, steep cliffs, or changing weather conditions. Follow designated paths and heed any posted warnings or advisories.

9.3 Tips for Navigating Public Transportation

Liguria's efficient and well-connected public transportation system makes exploring the region a breeze. Whether you're traveling between towns, embarking on scenic train journeys, or enjoying local buses, these tips will help you navigate the public transportation system with ease.

1. Plan Your Routes in Advance

Before setting out, familiarize yourself with the routes and schedules. Use reliable online resources, official transportation websites, or dedicated mobile apps for real-time updates and accurate information on routes, timetables, and ticket prices.

2. Ticketing and Validation

Always ensure you have a valid ticket before boarding public transportation. Tickets can typically be purchased at stations, kiosks, or online. In some cases, you may need to validate your ticket at designated machines before boarding to avoid fines.

3. Consider Multi-Use Cards or Passes

If you plan on using public transportation frequently, consider purchasing multi-use cards or passes. These options often provide cost savings compared to individual tickets and can be more convenient for hassle-free travel.

4. Understand the Different Transportation Modes

Liguria offers a range of transportation options, including trains, buses, trams, and ferries. Each mode of transport has its own unique routes and schedules, so be sure to understand the best option for your specific destination.

5. Trains: The Backbone of Ligurian Transportation

Trains are a popular and efficient way to travel between towns and cities in Liguria. The region boasts a well-maintained railway network, offering stunning coastal routes and easy access to the picturesque Cinque Terre villages. Familiarize yourself with the main train stations, and be sure to check the schedules for any changes or updates.

6. Local Buses: Urban and Inter-Town Travel

Liguria's local bus network is extensive, providing access to both urban centers and smaller towns. Be sure to check bus routes and schedules in advance, and have a clear understanding of the stops along your route. Bus stops are typically well-marked with schedules posted.

7. Ferries: Exploring Coastal Towns

If you're planning to visit coastal towns like Portofino or the Cinque Terre, consider utilizing the ferry services. These not only offer a scenic mode of transportation but also grant you breathtaking views of Liguria's picturesque coastline.

8. Taxis and Ride-Sharing Services

Taxis are readily available in urban areas and at transportation hubs. Make sure to use licensed and reputable taxi services. Alternatively, ride-sharing services may also be available in some areas.

9. Stay Informed About Strikes or Delays

Occasionally, public transportation services may be affected by strikes or unforeseen delays. Stay informed through official channels and consider having alternative plans in place if necessary.

10. Language Considerations

While English is widely understood in tourist areas, it can be helpful to learn a few basic Italian phrases for communication with locals and transportation staff. It's a gesture that's often appreciated and can enhance your overall experience.

9.4 Travel Insurance and its Importance

When embarking on a journey to the enchanting region of Liguria, Italy, the allure of picturesque coastlines, historic towns, and culinary delights often takes center stage in our thoughts. However, amidst the excitement of travel planning, it's crucial not to overlook a fundamental aspect of your trip: travel insurance. This invaluable safeguard offers peace of mind and financial protection in the face of unforeseen circumstances. Here, we'll explore the importance of travel insurance for tourists visiting Liguria and delve into the types of coverage to consider.

The Essence of Travel Insurance

Travel insurance acts as a safety net, providing a shield against a range of unexpected events that can disrupt or derail your travel plans. It offers a layer of financial protection, ensuring that you're not left bearing the full brunt of unforeseen expenses. From medical emergencies to trip cancellations, lost luggage to flight delays, travel insurance steps in to ease the burden, allowing you to focus on enjoying your Ligurian adventure.

Medical Emergencies: A Critical Consideration

One of the most vital aspects of travel insurance is its coverage of medical emergencies. While Liguria boasts an excellent healthcare system, unforeseen circumstances can arise, and the cost of medical treatment abroad can be substantial. Travel insurance ensures that you have access to quality healthcare without incurring exorbitant expenses. From minor ailments to more serious medical conditions, having comprehensive coverage can make all the difference.

Trip Cancellations and Interruptions: Safeguarding Your Investment

Imagine this scenario: You've meticulously planned your Ligurian itinerary, booked accommodations, and secured tickets to must-see attractions. Suddenly, an unexpected event forces you to cancel your trip or cut it short. This is where trip cancellation and interruption coverage proves invaluable. It reimburses you for non-refundable expenses, allowing you to recoup a significant portion of your investment. Whether it's due to a sudden illness, family emergency, or unforeseen circumstances, this coverage offers a financial safety net.

Baggage and Personal Belongings: Protecting Your Valuables

The loss, theft, or damage of luggage and personal belongings is an unfortunate but not uncommon occurrence in travel. Travel insurance steps in to provide coverage for such incidents, ensuring that you're not left stranded without essential items. This coverage extends to items like electronics, passports, jewelry, and more. Knowing that you have financial protection for your belongings can offer a tremendous sense of security.

Travel Delays and Missed Connections: Navigating Unexpected Hurdles

Travel doesn't always go according to plan. Flights can be delayed, connections missed, and itineraries disrupted. In such situations, travel insurance can help cover additional expenses incurred due to unexpected delays. This can include costs for accommodation, meals, and transportation while you wait for your journey to resume.

Adventure Activities Coverage: Tailoring to Your Pursuits

Liguria offers a diverse range of activities, from hiking the rugged Cinque Terre trails to exploring underwater wonders in the Ligurian Sea. If you plan to engage in adventurous pursuits, it's crucial to ensure your travel insurance covers any potential injuries related to these activities. This specialized coverage provides an extra layer of protection for adrenaline-fueled adventures.

Choosing the Right Policy: Tailoring Coverage to Your Needs

When selecting travel insurance for your Ligurian escapade, it's important to consider your specific needs and preferences. Assess the type of activities you'll be engaging in, the duration of your trip, and any potential health concerns. Be sure to read the policy details thoroughly, and don't hesitate to ask questions to ensure you have a clear understanding of the coverage provided.

CHAPTER TEN
ACCOMMODATION

10.1 Hotels and Resorts

Liguria offers a wide range of hotels and resorts catering to different tastes and budgets. From luxurious beachfront resorts in Santa Margherita Ligure to charming boutique hotels tucked away in the alleys of Cinque Terre, there's something for everyone. These accommodations provide amenities such as spa services, exquisite dining options, and breathtaking views of the Ligurian coast.

Recommend Hotels and Resorts with Their Locations

1. Grand Hotel Miramare

Location: Santa Margherita Ligure

Nestled along the serene Gulf of Tigullio, the Grand Hotel Miramare stands as a beacon of classic elegance harmoniously blended with modern comforts. This luxurious retreat in Santa Margherita Ligure offers discerning travelers an experience beyond compare. The moment you arrive, you're greeted by sweeping sea views that stretch as far as the eye can see. The lush gardens surrounding the property create an oasis of tranquility, inviting guests to unwind amidst nature's splendor.

Every aspect of the Grand Hotel Miramare is thoughtfully curated to provide an atmosphere of refined opulence. From the meticulously appointed rooms to the impeccable service, guests are treated to a world of lavish indulgence. Whether you choose to relax by the poolside, enjoy a leisurely stroll in the verdant gardens, or savor delectable cuisine at the hotel's restaurant, every moment is designed to leave an indelible mark.

2. Belmond Hotel Splendido

Location: Portofino

In the heart of the enchanting Portofino, the Belmond Hotel Splendido reigns supreme as a bastion of timeless luxury. This historic gem exudes an aura of grandeur, steeped in a rich heritage that dates back decades. From its vantage point, guests are treated to panoramic views that frame the azure expanse of the Mediterranean Sea. The opulent accommodations are a testament to meticulous attention to detail, ensuring that every guest feels like royalty.

What truly sets the Belmond Hotel Splendido apart is its Michelin-starred restaurant, where culinary artistry meets the freshest local ingredients. Dining here is an experience that transcends the ordinary, elevating the senses with each delectable dish. With every corner steeped in history and luxury, the Belmond Hotel Splendido is a sanctuary of indulgence for those seeking an extraordinary retreat.

3. Vernazza Rooms

Location: Vernazza, Cinque Terre

Nestled in the heart of Vernazza, one of the jewels of the Cinque Terre, Vernazza Rooms offers a warm and inviting haven with a distinct Italian charm. The comfortable rooms provide a cozy sanctuary after a day of exploring the vibrant streets and breathtaking coastal views. Here, guests have the privilege of immersing themselves in the authentic atmosphere of Cinque Terre, stepping out of their doorstep into a world of history, culture, and natural beauty.

4. Hotel Porto Roca

Location: Monterosso al Mare, Cinque Terre

Perched on the cliffs overlooking the Ligurian Sea, Hotel Porto Roca presents a mesmerizing tableau of coastal beauty. The breathtaking views of the rugged coastline and crystalline waters create an ambiance of unparalleled serenity. This family-run establishment seamlessly blends Mediterranean hospitality with modern amenities, ensuring that guests feel both at home and pampered.

Whether you're lounging by the infinity pool, indulging in a rejuvenating spa treatment, or savoring the regional delicacies at the hotel's restaurant, every moment at Hotel Porto Roca is an invitation to embrace the best of Cinque Terre's charm.

5. Hotel Vis à Vis

Location: Sestri Levante

Perched high above the Bay of Silence and the Bay of Fables, Hotel Vis à Vis offers a retreat of serenity and sweeping views. The elevated position of the hotel provides a unique vantage point for guests to soak in the breathtaking beauty of Sestri Levante and the Ligurian coastline. The rooftop terrace, with its unrivaled panoramas, becomes a sanctuary for witnessing the awe-inspiring sunsets over the shimmering sea.

6. Royal Hotel Sanremo

Location: Sanremo

Nestled amidst lush gardens along the Sanremo promenade, the Royal Hotel Sanremo stands as a testament to timeless elegance and historical significance. This graceful hotel offers a private beach, inviting guests to bask in the Mediterranean sun and sea. The top-notch spa facilities provide a haven of relaxation and rejuvenation. With its proximity to the city's attractions, guests can effortlessly explore the cultural riches of Sanremo while reveling in the opulence of this distinguished establishment.

10.2 Boutique Stays

For those seeking a more personalized and unique experience, boutique stays are an excellent choice. These intimate accommodations often reflect the local culture and history of Liguria. Imagine staying in a converted seaside villa with original frescoes or a family-run bed and breakfast nestled in the hills overlooking the Mediterranean. Boutique stays offer a warm and authentic atmosphere that larger hotels may not provide.

Recommend Boutique Stays with Their Locations

1. La Casa di Ulisse

Location: Riomaggiore, Cinque Terre

Nestled amidst the enchanting alleys of Riomaggiore, La Casa di Ulisse unveils an intimate haven for those seeking an authentic Cinque Terre experience. This boutique guesthouse, adorned with vibrant local artwork, exudes a welcoming atmosphere that wraps guests in the warmth of Ligurian hospitality. Each corner of La Casa di Ulisse is carefully curated to provide a sanctuary where weary travelers can unwind and rejuvenate after a day of exploration. Here, the essence of Cinque Terre's charm is captured, offering not just accommodation, but a true immersion into the heart of this coastal gem.

2. Ca' de Baran

Location: Portovenere

In the heart of Portovenere's historic center, Ca' de Baran stands as a charming testament to the essence of Ligurian coastal living. This boutique stay captures the very soul of its seaside surroundings, offering beautifully decorated rooms, some of which boast breathtaking sea views. Guests at Ca' de Baran are invited to step into the vibrant ambiance of Portovenere, where the scent of the sea mingles with the colors of the picturesque buildings, creating an unforgettable coastal retreat.

3. Agriturismo Le Pale

Location: Levanto

Amidst the verdant embrace of a thriving olive grove, Agriturismo Le Pale beckons as a serene retreat just a short drive from Levanto and the renowned Cinque Terre. This boutique agriturismo provides more than just a place to rest;

it offers an authentic farm-to-table experience. Guests have the opportunity to savor the rich, genuine flavors of Liguria, directly from the land to their plates. The comfortable rooms and tranquil surroundings make Agriturismo Le Pale a haven of rustic charm and natural beauty.

4. Villa Rosmarino

Location: Camogli

Perched above the captivating fishing village of Camogli, Villa Rosmarino unveils the beauty of a lovingly restored 19th-century villa turned boutique bed and breakfast. The elegant rooms, adorned with period furnishings, offer a glimpse into Liguria's rich maritime history. From this vantage point, guests can soak in the spectacular views of the Ligurian Sea and the colorful houses cascading down the hillside. Villa Rosmarino is not merely a place to stay; it is an invitation to step back in time and relish the timeless allure of the Italian Riviera.

5. La Malà

Location: Noli

Tucked away within the medieval walls of Noli, La Malà seamlessly weaves history with contemporary design. This boutique guesthouse presents a collection of stylish rooms, each uniquely decorated to offer a distinctive experience. As guests step out onto the charming streets of Noli, they are greeted by the echoes of centuries past, a testament to the enduring spirit of this coastal town. La Malà is a refuge for those seeking a blend of heritage and modern comfort in the heart of Liguria.

6. Locanda Ca' dei Duxi

Location: Manarola, Cinque Terre

In the heart of Manarola, one of the iconic Cinque Terre villages, Locanda Ca' dei Duxi beckons with its cozy rooms and captivating sea views. This boutique stay invites guests to immerse themselves in the authentic charm of the village, where the scent of the sea mingles with the vibrant colors of the buildings perched on the cliffs. From Locanda Ca' dei Duxi, guests can embark on explorations of the stunning coastal trails, each step a testament to the natural beauty that defines this corner of Liguria.

10.3 Budget-Friendly Options

Travelers on a budget need not worry about finding comfortable and affordable lodging in Liguria. There are numerous budget-friendly options available, including hostels, guesthouses, and budget hotels. While these accommodations may offer fewer frills compared to luxury resorts, they still provide clean and comfortable rooms, making them a perfect choice for travelers looking to maximize their exploration without breaking the bank.

Recommend Budget-Friendly with Their Locations

1. A Ca' Da Nonna

Location: Vernazza, Cinque Terre

Nestled amidst the enchanting alleys of Vernazza, one of Cinque Terre's most picturesque villages, A Ca' Da Nonna embodies the true essence of Ligurian hospitality. This family-run guesthouse exudes a unique charm, offering guests not just a place to stay, but an immersive experience in the heart of Vernazza's vibrant community. The comfortable rooms, adorned with local touches, provide a cozy retreat after a day of exploration along the rugged coastline. The scent of the sea and the colorful facades of Vernazza's houses permeate the air, creating an atmosphere of pure coastal enchantment.

2. La Casa di Ale

Location: Monterosso al Mare, Cinque Terre

Perched in the heart of Monterosso al Mare, La Casa di Ale extends a warm welcome to travelers seeking a comfortable and well-appointed retreat. This welcoming guesthouse offers a sanctuary of calm just moments away from the beach. The convenience of its location allows guests to easily explore the lively streets of this coastal town. After a day of sun-soaked adventures, guests can return to the cozy embrace of La Casa di Ale, where comfort and hospitality are woven into every corner.

3. Ostello Porto Venere

Location: Portovenere

For the budget-conscious traveler, Ostello Porto Venere stands as a reliable choice in the heart of Portovenere. This hostel offers comfortable dormitory-style accommodation, providing a practical base for exploring the historic town and its awe-inspiring surroundings. From the hostel's doorstep, guests can immerse themselves in the rich history of Portovenere and gaze upon the breathtaking Gulf of Poets. The hostel's communal atmosphere encourages interactions with fellow travelers, creating a sense of camaraderie and shared adventure.

4. Hostel 5 Terre

Location: Manarola, Cinque Terre

Nestled in the heart of Manarola, one of the iconic villages of Cinque Terre, Hostel 5 Terre beckons with its affordability and friendly ambiance. The hostel provides dormitory-style rooms where guests can rest and recharge, ready for the next day's exploration. With its prime location, it serves as an excellent base for hikers and nature enthusiasts eager to traverse the trails and experience the rugged beauty of Cinque Terre National Park. The communal spaces foster connections among guests, making for a memorable and enriching stay.

5. B&B La Costa

Location: Levanto

In the coastal town of Levanto, B&B La Costa offers a cozy and welcoming retreat just a stone's throw from the sandy shores and the train station. The comfortable rooms, adorned with thoughtful details, create a pleasant atmosphere for guests to unwind and savor their Ligurian experience. The hosts, with their warm hospitality, add a personal touch to the stay, ensuring that every guest feels right at home in this coastal haven.

6. Hostel Noli

Location: Noli

Immersed in the medieval charm of Noli, Hostel Noli provides a budget-friendly option for travelers seeking affordability without sacrificing comfort. The hostel offers dormitory-style rooms and a communal kitchen, creating a social atmosphere for guests to share their travel experiences. Nestled within the historic streets and a short stroll from the beaches, Hostel Noli invites guests to soak in the rich history and natural beauty of this coastal gem. It's a perfect choice for those looking to make the most of their Ligurian adventure.

10.4 Unique Accommodation Experiences

For travelers seeking to infuse their Ligurian sojourn with a touch of magic, the region offers a selection of extraordinary lodgings that transcend the conventional. These distinctive accommodations promise not just a place to rest, but an experience to cherish. Imagine spending the night in a converted lighthouse, perched sentinel-like on the rugged Ligurian coastline, or finding solace in a traditional Italian trullo, nestled amidst the boughs of an ancient olive grove. These one-of-a-kind lodgings invite guests to weave their own tales of adventure and create indelible memories in the embrace of Liguria's awe-inspiring landscapes.

1. Lighthouse Retreat, Portovenere

Location: Portovenere

Set against the backdrop of Portovenere's dramatic coastline, the Lighthouse Retreat offers a stay like no other. Housed within a meticulously converted historic lighthouse, this unique accommodation provides panoramic views of the

Gulf of Poets. The rhythmic sweep of the lighthouse beam and the soothing sound of waves against the cliffs create an atmosphere of unparalleled tranquility. Guests have the rare opportunity to step into the shoes of a lighthouse keeper, immersing themselves in the maritime heritage of Liguria.

2. Trullo Hideaway, Imperia

Location: Imperia

Nestled within an ancient olive grove in Imperia, the Trullo Hideaway offers a rustic yet luxurious retreat. This traditional Italian trullo, with its conical stone roof and whitewashed walls, provides a unique blend of heritage and comfort. The scent of olive trees and the song of cicadas surround guests, creating an ambiance of pure Mediterranean serenity. The Trullo Hideaway is a haven for those seeking to disconnect from the bustle of modern life and reconnect with the natural rhythms of Liguria.

3. Castle Stay, Dolceacqua

Location: Dolceacqua

Perched atop a hill in the charming village of Dolceacqua, the Castle Stay transports guests back in time to an era of medieval splendor. This meticulously restored castle offers a truly regal experience, with elegantly furnished rooms and sweeping views of the Nervia Valley. Guests can wander through the ancient halls, explore the castle's gardens, and savor the romance of a bygone era. The Castle Stay is an enchanting destination for history enthusiasts and those seeking a fairy tale escape.

4. Olive Mill Retreat, Levanto

Location: Levanto

In the heart of Levanto, a unique accommodation awaits in the form of an Olive Mill Retreat. Housed within a meticulously restored olive mill, this boutique lodging offers a blend of history and modern comfort. Guests can marvel at the preserved mill machinery while enjoying the contemporary amenities provided. The Olive Mill Retreat provides a glimpse into the rich agricultural heritage of Liguria, all while being just a short walk from the beach and the vibrant town center.

5. Cliffside Cottage, Bonassola

Location: Bonassola

Perched dramatically on the cliffs overlooking the Ligurian Sea, the Cliffside Cottage in Bonassola offers a secluded and breathtaking escape. This charming cottage, with its panoramic terrace, provides an unrivaled vantage point for witnessing the sun's descent into the horizon. The sound of waves crashing against the rocks below and the salty sea breeze create an immersive coastal experience. The Cliffside Cottage is a haven for those seeking serenity and unspoiled natural beauty.

6. Treehouse Retreat, La Spezia

Location: La Spezia

For a truly unique and immersive experience, consider a stay in a Treehouse Retreat in the hills surrounding La Spezia. These elevated lodgings offer a bird's eye view of the lush

Ligurian countryside, creating a sense of being cradled by nature itself. The rustling leaves and symphony of birdsong provide a soundtrack to this arboreal escape. The Treehouse Retreat is a testament to the harmonious coexistence between man and the natural world, offering an unforgettable stay in Liguria.

These extraordinary accommodations in Liguria provide more than just a place to lay one's head—they offer a canvas for crafting unforgettable moments in the embrace of this captivating region. Each stay promises a unique journey, where the setting itself becomes an integral part of the travel narrative. Whether perched in a lighthouse, nestled in an olive grove, or ensconced in a medieval castle, these lodgings invite guests to create their own stories against the backdrop of Liguria's incomparable beauty.

10.5 Tips for Finding the Right Lodging for Your Needs

1. Define Your Priorities

Before you start searching for accommodation, make a list of your priorities. Are you looking for a beachfront property, a central location, or a tranquil retreat in the countryside? Knowing what matters most to you will help narrow down your options.

2. Consider Your Budget

Set a budget range for accommodation. This will help you filter out options that are too expensive and focus on places that align with your budget. Remember to factor in any additional costs like taxes, fees, and potential amenities.

3. Research Different Areas

Liguria offers diverse landscapes, from coastal towns to inland villages. Research the different areas to find the one that best suits your interests. For instance, if you want a lively atmosphere and easy beach access, focus on the towns along the Riviera. If you prefer a quieter experience, look into the charming villages nestled in the hills.

4. Read Reviews and Ratings

Websites and platforms like TripAdvisor, Booking.com, and Airbnb provide valuable insights from fellow travelers. Pay attention to reviews mentioning factors important to you, such as cleanliness, amenities, and location. This can give you a clearer picture of what to expect.

5. Check Amenities and Services

Different accommodations offer varying amenities. Consider whether you need features like Wi-Fi, on-site dining, a pool, or a kitchenette. Make a list of must-haves and nice-to-haves to help narrow down your options.

6. Contact the Accommodation Directly

If you have specific questions or requests, don't hesitate to reach out to the accommodation directly. They can provide additional information and may even offer special arrangements to make your stay more comfortable.

7. Use Map Views

Many booking platforms allow you to view accommodations on a map. This can help you understand the proximity of your chosen lodging to key attractions, public transport, and other points of interest.

8. Consider Booking Flexibility

Given unforeseen circumstances, it's wise to choose accommodation with flexible cancellation policies. This way, if your plans change, you won't be stuck with a non-refundable reservation.

9. Look for Special Offers or Packages

Some accommodations offer special deals or packages that can enhance your stay. This could include discounted rates for extended stays, complimentary breakfast, or access to exclusive amenities.

10. Trust Your Instincts

Ultimately, go with your gut feeling. If a particular accommodation resonates with you and checks off most of your criteria, it's likely a good fit.

CHAPTER ELEVEN

LIGURIA TRAVEL ITINERARIES

11.1 One-Week Highlights Tour

Day 1: Arrival in Genoa

Your Ligurian adventure begins as you touch down at Genoa Cristoforo Colombo Airport. From here, make your way to your chosen accommodation in the heart of the city. After settling in, embark on a leisurely stroll through Genoa's historic Old Town, known as the "Caruggi," a labyrinth of narrow alleys and charming squares. Don't miss the chance to savor some authentic Genoese pesto in one of the local trattorias.

Day 2: Genoa's Maritime Majesty

Dedicate your second day to exploring Genoa's maritime heritage. Start with a visit to the Acquario di Genova, one of Europe's largest aquariums. Afterward, explore the Old Port area and visit the Galata Maritime Museum, where you'll learn about Genoa's seafaring history. In the afternoon, take a panoramic elevator ride to the top of "Bigo," offering spectacular views of the city.

Day 3: Day Trip to Portofino

Board a regional train and in just 30 minutes, you'll arrive in the glamorous village of Portofino. Enjoy a day of indulgence in this charming harbor town. Explore the Piazzetta, visit Castello Brown for stunning vistas, and savor fresh seafood in one of the picturesque restaurants. For nature enthusiasts, consider hiking to the San Fruttuoso Abbey or exploring the nearby Regional Natural Park.

Day 4: Santa Margherita Ligure and Rapallo

Spend the morning in Santa Margherita Ligure, a delightful coastal town just a short train ride from Genoa. Enjoy the scenic waterfront promenade, shop for souvenirs, and relax on the sandy beach. In the afternoon, venture to Rapallo, another charming coastal gem. Explore the historic center and perhaps take a boat ride to the secluded San Michele di Pagana beach.

Day 5: The Cinque Terre - Monterosso and Vernazza

Start your Cinque Terre exploration with a trip to Monterosso al Mare, the largest of the five villages. Relax on the beautiful beaches, and explore the historic old town. In the afternoon, hop on a short train ride to Vernazza. This iconic village is known for its colorful buildings and picturesque harbor. Hike the trails or simply savor local seafood while admiring the breathtaking views.

Day 6: The Cinque Terre - Corniglia, Manarola, and Riomaggiore

Dedicate this day to visiting the remaining three Cinque Terre villages. Begin with Corniglia, perched on a hilltop with spectacular panoramas. Continue to Manarola, a charming village known for its wine production, and explore the scenic trails. Finish the day in Riomaggiore, the southernmost village, with its narrow streets and charming atmosphere.

Day 7: Farewell to Liguria

On your final day, take a leisurely morning stroll in Genoa, soaking in any last-minute sights or shopping for souvenirs. Depending on your departure time, you might want to enjoy one last Ligurian meal at a local restaurant. Bid farewell to Liguria as you make your way to the airport, cherishing the memories of a week filled with stunning coastal views, rich history, and delectable cuisine.

This one-week highlights tour provides a taste of Liguria's diverse and captivating attractions. Of course, Liguria has much more to offer, so consider returning to explore further or delve into specific interests like hiking, culinary adventures, or historical explorations.

11.2 Family-Friendly Adventure

Day 1: Monterosso al Mare

- Morning: Arrive in Monterosso al Mare, the northernmost village of Cinque Terre. Spend the day on the beautiful beach, building sandcastles and swimming in the clear waters.
- Afternoon: Stroll along the seaside promenade and explore the charming old town. Visit the Church of San Giovanni Battista and savor local gelato.
- Evening: Enjoy a family-friendly dinner at a seaside trattoria.

Day 2: Vernazza and Boat Excursion

- Morning: Take a short train ride to Vernazza. Explore the colorful village, visit the Doria Castle, and enjoy a family hike on the scenic trail to Monterosso.
- Afternoon: Embark on a boat excursion to see Cinque Terre from the sea. Discover hidden coves and swim in the crystal-clear Mediterranean.
- Evening: Return to Monterosso for a relaxing evening by the beach.

Day 3: Corniglia and Scenic Train Ride

- Morning: Catch a train to Corniglia, the only village not directly on the water. Enjoy panoramic views from the terraced vineyards and explore the charming town.
- Afternoon: Take a leisurely hike to Manarola along the famous Via dell'Amore trail. Stop for a family picnic along the way.
- Evening: Experience a traditional Ligurian dinner in Manarola.

Day 4: Manarola and Riomaggiore

- Morning: Explore Manarola's picturesque streets and visit the Manarola Scenic Viewpoint for breathtaking coastal vistas.
- Afternoon: Take a short train ride to Riomaggiore. Explore the historic center and relax by the water.
- Evening: Enjoy a seafood dinner at a family-friendly restaurant in Riomaggiore.

Week 2: Genoa's Maritime Magic

Day 5: Exploring Genoa's Old Town

- Morning: Arrive in Genoa and head to the historic Old Town. Visit the Genoa Cathedral and explore the narrow streets lined with vibrant shops.
- Afternoon: Discover the Palazzo Reale and the Galata Maritime Museum. Take a family-friendly guided tour to learn about Genoa's maritime history.
- Evening: Dine in a family-friendly trattoria in the heart of the Old Town.

Day 6: The Port of Genoa and Aquarium

- Morning: Spend the morning at the bustling Port of Genoa. Visit the Bigo Panoramic Lift for a spectacular view of the port.
- Afternoon: Explore the Genoa Aquarium, one of the largest aquariums in Europe. Marvel at the diverse marine life and enjoy interactive exhibits for kids.
- Evening: Take a leisurely stroll along the Porto Antico, enjoying street performers and local gelato.

Day 7: Day Trips from Genoa

- Morning: Choose from family-friendly day trip options such as a visit to the charming village of Portofino or a scenic boat ride to the Gulf of Poets.
- Afternoon: Explore the chosen destination, indulging in activities like hiking, swimming, or simply soaking in the coastal beauty.

- Evening: Return to Genoa and celebrate your last night with a special family dinner.

This two-week itinerary provides a balanced mix of coastal exploration in Cinque Terre and cultural immersion in Genoa, ensuring a memorable family adventure in Liguria. Remember to adjust the schedule based on your family's preferences and the specific interests of your travelers.

11.3 Solo Traveler's Journey

Day 1: Arrival in Genoa

Your solo adventure in Liguria begins in the historic port city of Genoa. After arriving at Genoa Cristoforo Colombo Airport, make your way to your chosen accommodation. Depending on your arrival time, spend your afternoon exploring Genoa's Old Town. Stroll through narrow alleyways, discover ancient palaces, and visit the iconic Genoa Aquarium. End the day with a taste of Ligurian cuisine at a local trattoria.

Day 2: Genoa's Historical Treasures

Start your day with a visit to the Palazzo Ducale, a historic palace with art exhibitions and cultural events. Explore the Old Port area, then head to Via Garibaldi, a UNESCO World Heritage site known for its stunning palaces. Spend the evening savoring local dishes in the Caruggi district, Genoa's culinary heart.

Day 3: Day Trip to Portofino

Take a day trip to the picturesque fishing village of Portofino, a short train or boat ride from Genoa. Wander through the charming streets, visit Castello Brown for panoramic views, and enjoy a relaxing afternoon by the harbor. Return to Genoa in the evening.

Day 4: Cinque Terre - Monterosso al Mare

Head to Monterosso al Mare, the northernmost village of the Cinque Terre. Explore the historic center, indulge in fresh seafood, and soak up the sun on the beach. Consider taking a hike to Vernazza or relaxing on the local hiking trails.

Day 5: Cinque Terre - Vernazza and Corniglia

Start your day with a visit to Vernazza, a picturesque village with a charming harbor. Afterward, take a train or hike to Corniglia, the smallest and most serene of the Cinque Terre villages. Enjoy local wine and take in the stunning views of the sea.

Day 6: Cinque Terre - Manarola and Riomaggiore

Explore Manarola, famous for its colorful buildings, then continue to Riomaggiore, known for its picturesque cove. Explore the historic paths and hidden corners of these two beautiful villages, and don't forget to try some local pesto.

Day 7: Cinque Terre - Hiking and Farewell

Your last day in Cinque Terre can be devoted to hiking. Consider the breathtaking coastal trail that connects all five villages. After completing your hike, savor a farewell dinner in the Cinque Terre, celebrating your memorable solo journey.

Day 8: Departure from Cinque Terre

Bid farewell to Cinque Terre and head back to Genoa. Depending on your departure time, you may have some time to explore any remaining Genoese sites or do some last-minute souvenir shopping before heading to the airport.

11.4 Romantic Getaways

Day 1: Arrival in Portofino

- Morning: Arrive in the picturesque town of Portofino, known for its colorful houses and stunning harbor views.
- Afternoon: Stroll along the waterfront promenade, visit Castello Brown, and have a romantic lunch overlooking the bay.
- Evening: Enjoy a candlelit dinner at a charming local restaurant.

Day 2: Santa Margherita Ligure

- Morning: Take a short boat ride to Santa Margherita Ligure, a lovely town with a lively atmosphere and beautiful beaches.
- Afternoon: Explore the historic center, visit the San Giacomo Church, and relax on the sandy shores.
- Evening: Dine at a seafront trattoria, savoring fresh seafood and local specialties.

Day 3: Hiking in Portofino Natural Park

- Morning: Embark on a romantic hike in the Portofino Natural Park, enjoying breathtaking views of the coastline.

- Afternoon: Have a leisurely picnic in the park or return to Portofino for a spa afternoon.
- Evening: Delight in a sunset aperitivo overlooking the sea.

Day 4: Rapallo and Sestri Levante

- Morning: Head to Rapallo and explore the historic town center, including the waterfront promenade and the castle.
- Afternoon: Continue to Sestri Levante, a charming seaside town, for a romantic beachfront afternoon.
- Evening: Dine in a cozy restaurant with sea views.

Week 2: The Romance of Cinque Terre

Day 5: Monterosso al Mare

- Morning: Travel to Monterosso al Mare, the largest of the Cinque Terre villages, and enjoy the beach and vibrant town center.
- Afternoon: Discover the hidden gems of the town, including the Convent of Monterosso and the Capuchin Monastery.
- Evening: Savor a romantic dinner at a local trattoria.

Day 6: Vernazza and Corniglia

- Morning: Explore Vernazza, a postcard-perfect village, and its beautiful harbor.
- Afternoon: Head to Corniglia, a quieter village perched on a hill, for stunning views and a serene atmosphere.

- Evening: Dine in a cozy restaurant with a romantic ambiance.

Day 7: Riomaggiore and Manarola

- Morning: Visit Riomaggiore, the southernmost village, known for its colorful houses and stunning views.
- Afternoon: Discover Manarola, a charming village with a picturesque harbor and excellent hiking trails.
- Evening: Enjoy a farewell dinner with a view of the Ligurian Sea.

Note: Depending on your travel goals as stated in chapter one of this travel guide and the type of travel itinerary you would like to go for, you can still add some places you would like to visit which were not included in your choice travel itinerary, you can adjust any of them to suit your travel goals so as to a have an enjoyable and memorable trip.

CHAPTER TWELVE
PRACTICAL TIPS AND RESOURCES

12.1 Local Phrases and Vocabulary

When exploring Liguria, it's always appreciated by locals when visitors make an effort to speak a bit of the local language. Here are some basic Italian phrases and vocabulary that can come in handy:

Greetings:

- Hello: Ciao
- Good morning: Buongiorno
- Good evening: Buonasera
- Good night: Buonanotte

Common Expressions:

- Thank you: Grazie
- Please: Per favore
- Excuse me / Sorry: Scusa / Mi dispiace
- Yes: Sì / No: No

Basic Questions:

- Where is...?: Dov'è...?
- How much is this?: Quanto costa questo?
- Can you help me?: Puoi aiutarmi?

Food and Drink:

- Menu: Menù
- Water: Acqua
- Wine: Vino
- Delicious: Delizioso

Numbers:

One: Uno / Two: Due / Three: Tre / Four: Quattro / Five: Cinque

Six: Sei / Seven: Sette / Eight: Otto / Nine: Nove / Ten: Dieci

Remember, don't be shy to try out these phrases, even if your pronunciation isn't perfect. The locals will appreciate your effort!

12.2 Emergency Contacts

In case of any emergencies during your stay in Liguria, here are some important contact numbers to keep in mind:

- Emergency Services (Police, Fire, Medical): 112
- Local Police (Carabinieri): 112
- Ambulance / Medical Emergency: 118
- Fire Department (Vigili del Fuoco): 115
- Coast Guard (Guardia Costiera): 1530

Note: Make sure to provide your exact location and describe the situation clearly when calling for emergency assistance.

12.3 Sustainable Travel Practices

Liguria's natural beauty is a treasure that deserves to be protected for future generations to enjoy. As responsible travelers, it is our duty to be stewards of this stunning coastal paradise. Here are some sustainable travel practices that you should keep in mind:

1. Reducing Plastic Use:

One of the simplest yet most impactful ways to reduce your environmental footprint is by carrying a reusable water bottle and shopping bag. This small change can significantly minimize the amount of single-use plastic waste in the region. By doing so, you help keep the picturesque landscapes of Liguria clean and free of plastic pollution.

2. Respecting Nature:

When exploring Liguria's natural wonders, always stick to designated trails and paths. Avoid wandering off the beaten track, as this can disturb local wildlife and ecosystems. Never pick plants or flowers, as it disrupts the delicate balance of the environment and can impact the biodiversity of the region.

3. Conserving Water:

In areas with limited water resources, it's essential to be mindful of your water usage. Simple actions like turning off taps when not in use and taking shorter showers can make a significant difference. Water conservation is crucial in ensuring the sustainability of the region's natural beauty.

4. Supporting Local Businesses:

Opt for locally-owned accommodations, restaurants, and shops. Not only does this provide a more authentic experience, but it also contributes to the local economy. By supporting local businesses, you help strengthen the community and promote sustainable tourism.

5. Using Public Transportation:

Consider using trains or buses instead of private cars for your travel within Liguria. Public transportation not only reduces the carbon footprint of your journey but also allows you to enjoy the scenic beauty of the region without the hassle of traffic and parking.

6. Proper Waste Disposal:

Always use designated recycling bins and follow local waste disposal guidelines. Proper waste disposal helps keep the environment clean and minimizes the impact of tourism on the region's natural landscapes.

In Liguria, these small, conscious actions can collectively make a substantial impact on preserving its beauty for generations to come. By practicing sustainable travel, you contribute to the long-term health and vitality of this coastal paradise.

12.4 Health Precautions

While Liguria is a generally safe and welcoming destination, it's important to prioritize your well-being during your visit. Here are some essential health precautions to consider:

- Stay Hydrated: Liguria's Mediterranean climate can be warm, especially in the summer months. Make sure to carry a refillable water bottle and drink plenty of fluids to stay hydrated, especially if you're engaging in outdoor activities.

- Sun Protection: The sun's rays can be strong, especially during peak hours. Apply sunscreen with a high SPF, wear a wide-brimmed hat, and consider sunglasses to protect yourself from harmful UV radiation.
- Insect Protection: If you're venturing into wooded or coastal areas, consider using insect repellent to guard against mosquito bites. This is especially important during dusk and dawn when insects tend to be more active.
- Medical Services: Familiarize yourself with the location of local hospitals, clinics, and pharmacies in case of any unexpected medical issues. The emergency number in Italy is 118.
- Travel Insurance: It's recommended to have comprehensive travel insurance that covers medical emergencies. This ensures you have access to healthcare services if the need arises.
- Food Safety: While Liguria is known for its delicious cuisine, it's important to exercise caution with food and water. Opt for reputable restaurants and avoid consuming raw or undercooked seafood.
- Prescription Medications: If you require prescription medications, ensure you have an adequate supply for the duration of your trip. It's also wise to carry a copy of your prescription in case it's needed.
- Footwear for Exploration: If you plan on exploring natural areas or embarking on hiking trails, sturdy, comfortable footwear is essential to prevent injuries and ensure a safe adventure.

- Emergency Contacts: Keep a list of important contacts, including local emergency numbers, your accommodation's contact information, and any relevant medical contacts.

By taking these health precautions into account, you'll be better equipped to enjoy your visit to Liguria while ensuring your well-being throughout your journey.

CONCLUSION

Reflecting on Your Ligurian Journey

As you approach the end of your adventure through Liguria, take a moment to pause and reflect on the memories you've created in this enchanting region. The sights, sounds, and flavors of Liguria have left an indelible mark on your travel experience.

Consider the picturesque villages of Cinque Terre, with their pastel-hued buildings clinging to the rugged cliffs. Recall the taste of fresh seafood and pesto, enjoyed in family-run trattorias overlooking the azure sea. Picture the historic alleys of Genoa, where tales of maritime glory are etched into every cobblestone.

Perhaps you found solace in the quiet charm of Portofino and Santa Margherita Ligure, or explored the lesser-known corners of the Riviera di Levante and Riviera di Ponente, discovering hidden beaches and centuries-old traditions.

The hinterland, with its rugged mountains and ancient villages, offered a glimpse into Liguria's rich cultural tapestry. Olive groves stretched as far as the eye could see, their gnarled trunks bearing witness to centuries of history.

As you reflect on your Ligurian journey, consider the connections forged with locals and fellow travelers. The shared moments of awe at the breathtaking landscapes, the laughter over shared meals, and the exchanges of stories and experiences.

Remember, your Ligurian adventure doesn't end here. The memories you've gathered are a treasure trove of inspiration for future travels. Whether it's revisiting the Ligurian coast or exploring new horizons, let this journey be a source of joy and wanderlust.

Take a moment to jot down your thoughts, impressions, and the moments that touched your heart. These reflections will serve as a cherished memento, a testament to the beauty and magic of Liguria, a coastal paradise that will forever hold a special place in your travel repertoire.

As you bid farewell to Liguria, carry with you the essence of this coastal paradise - the warmth of its people, the splendor of its landscapes, and the timeless allure of its culture. Until we meet again, may your travels be filled with discovery, wonder, and the enduring spirit of adventure.

Printed in Great Britain
by Amazon